Do you know...
the most
Scary, Hairy,
Creepy
Insects
and Spiders
... in the World?

Bounty
Books

First published in 2009 by Bounty Books,
a division of Octopus Publishing Group Ltd.
2–4 Heron Quays, London E14 4JP

An Hachette Livre UK Company

A BROWN REFERENCE GROUP BOOK
Devised and produced by The Brown Reference Group plc,
8 Chapel Place, Rivington Street, London EC2A 3DQ
www.brownreference.com

ISBN-13: 978-0-753716-70-0

For The Brown Reference Group plc
Author: Tom Jackson
Designer: Dave Allen
Picture Researcher: Clare Newman
Managing Editor: Bridget Giles
Creative Director: Jeni Child
Editorial Director: Lindsey Lowe

PHOTOGRAPHIC CREDITS
Front Cover: Shutterstock: Coko
Title Page: Shutterstock: Tomasz Pietryszek
ARS: Scott Bauer 27, 80t, Rob Flynn 80b, Peggy Greb 31b; **Center for Disease Control & Prevention:** 16, James Gatlany 15; **Photos.com:** 7, 22t, 144b, 152b, 156, 198; **Shutterstock:** 37, 168, 204b, David Acosta Allely 188, Alle 54t, 131, Anastazzo 204t, Vadym Andrushchenko 169, Sue Ashe 48, Aurelio 164, Maciek Baran 118, John Bell 175, 179, 180, 195, Stephanie Bidouze 8, Casey K. Bishop 207, Aleksander Bolbot, 146, Stephen Bonk 103, Miles Boyer 191, Alex James Bramwell 102t, Ariel Bravy 46b, Michael Bretherton 54b, Joseph Calev 50b, 141t, 154, Karla Caspari 150, Ronald Caswell 82, 97, Sergey Chushkin 88, 89, 107bl, Hirleesteanu Constantin-Ciprian 33b, Kurt De Bruyn 139, Roger Devenish Jones 12, Maslov Dmitry 92t, David Dohnal 202, EcoPrint 166, 196, Stale Edstrom 64, Dean Evangelista 34, 87b, Alexey Evsyunin 101, Jip Fens 51, Florida Stock 6, Lori Froeb 104b, Jurgita Genyta 112, Daniel Gilbrey 121, Jarno Gonzales Zarraonandia 29, Joe Gough 78, Tom Grundy 111t, 147, Peter Gudella 171, Robert Hardholt 90, Chris Harvey 14, Lukas Hejtman 38, Bjorn Heller 20, 115, Rogello Hernandez Morales 71b, Michael Hiler 113, Ron Hilton 30, Moroslav Hlavko 63, Christopher David Howells 107t, Jhaz Photography 163, Jocicalek 41, Adrian T. Jones 120, 141b, Alex Kapranoff 47b, Sebastian Kaulitzhi 206t, Cathy Keifer 85, 99b, 114b, 161t, 161b, 176, 185, Ra'id Khalil 149b, 152t, Falk Kienas 32, Kmitu 31t, James A. Kost 137, Emily Kun 106b, Goran Kuzmanovski 145, K. R. Lena 194, Lisette Lewis 184, Paula P. Lewis 173, Lezh 59, Hway Kiong Lim 50t, 187, 199, Willie Linn 127b, Luis Louro 160, Macro Lens 87t, Maggie 83t, William Maher 98, Thomas Mansey 33t, Roxanne McMullen 96, Steve McWilliam 18, 104t, 107br, 111b, 119, 129, 158, Christopher Meder 193, Rodney Mehring 126, 132t, 132b, Michelle D. Milliman 43, Martina Misar 128, Paul B. Moore 42, Ryan Morgan 79, Andre Moritz 159, Nirdesha Munasinghe 144t, Kim Murrell 52, Christian Musat 72, 86b, Andre Nantel 133t, Keith Naylor 57b, Regien Paassen 35, Philip Pang Chee Seng 138, Varina & Jay Patel 66, Mark William Penny 135, Michael Pettigrew 17, 60, 71t, 142b, 205t, Photomedia.com 77, Thomasz Pietryszek 13, Pixelman 56, 57t, 92c, Alexander Potapov 149t, Jan Quist 76b, Radu Razvan 53b, Dr. Morley Read 143, 200b, Laurent Renault 91b, Lawrence Roberg 22b, Steve Shap 21, 65, Ronald Sherwood 94, Sheve Shoup 142t, 162, Siloto 93, Lori Skelton 83c, Carolina K. Smith, M.D. 172, Michael G. Smith 106t, Gladyshova Sofiya 127t, Joy Stein 109, Priscilla R. Stelle 53t, Paula Stephens 47t, Margaret M. Stewart 114t, Jens Stolt 124, Amos Struch 205b, Studio Araminta 40, Johan Swanepoel 76t, Brad Thompson 99t, Richard Thornton 143, Irina Tischenko 102b, Florin Tirlea 133b, 136, Suzanne Tucker 206b, Chris Turner 125, Dariusz Urbanczyk 36, Joris Van Den Heuvel 192, Stefanie Vander Vinder 86t, Emily Veinglory 46t, Ismael Montero Verdu 178, Mike Von Bergen 140, Chrstopher Waters 108, David Woods 44, Judy Worley 84, 200t, Yaroslav 117, Frank B. Yuwono 203, Artur Zinatulin 91t, Joanna Zopoth-Lipiejko 67, Tim Zurowski 95, 100, 105, 167.

Printed and bound in China

Contents

CHAPTER 1
GRASSHOPPERS & CRICKETS

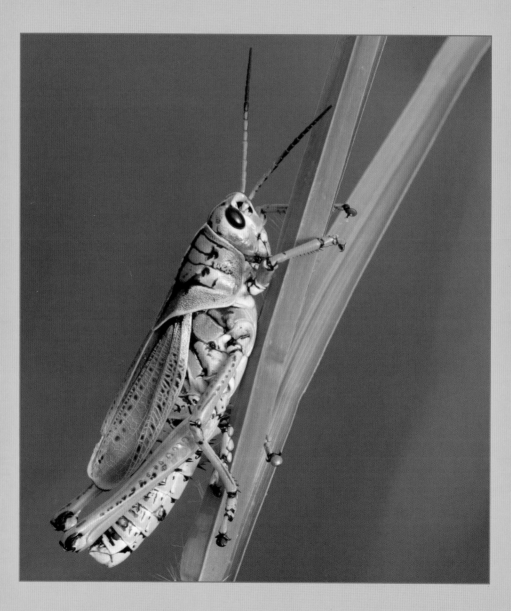

How do katydids stay hidden?

A katydid disguised as a leaf.

Katydids are crickets with long antennae, or feelers. They are named after the sound of their calls. They call by making a series of clicks that sound a bit like someone saying, "Katy did! Katy didn't!"

Katydids are nocturnal; that is, they are active at night. Most of them eat plants and spend their nights munching on leaves. Several katydids have a clever way of staying hidden from hunters – they pretend to be leaves themselves. The insects' long front wings are green and leaf shaped. The wings also have a pattern of branched lines that makes them look just like the surfaces of leaves.

Do you know...?

Some katydids pretend to be dead leaves, so they have brown wings instead of green. If the disguise fails, the katydid spreads its wings to fly away. The hind wings, which are normally hidden under the front wings, have colourful spots on them. The spots look like eyes and surprise an attacker for long enough for the insect to escape.

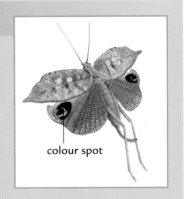

colour spot

What's the difference between a cricket and a grasshopper?

Crickets and grasshoppers form a group of insects called the orthopterans. The name orthopteran means 'straight wing', and all grasshoppers and crickets have two pairs of long, narrow wings that stretch along the length of their backs. However, there are several differences between the two types of insect. Grasshoppers have short antennae, or feelers, that point forwards. A cricket's antennae are longer and thinner, and they often sweep back over the insect's body. Strange as it may sound, crickets have ears on their legs, while grasshoppers hear through their sides. And finally, as their name suggests, grasshoppers have longer back legs than crickets, so they can make giant leaps.

A grasshopper sits on a leaf.

Do you know...?

A tree cricket cuts a body-sized hole in a leaf and then fits itself into it. When the cricket sings, or makes rasping calls, the leaf acts like a loudspeaker to broadcast the noise throughout the forest.

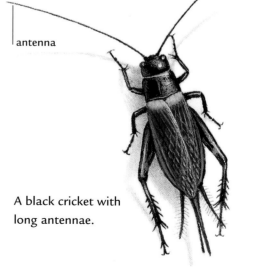

antenna

A black cricket with long antennae.

How do wetas survive being frozen solid?

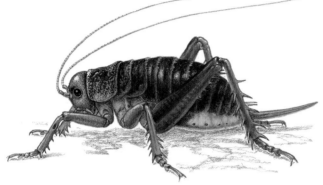

A Stephens Island weta from southern New Zealand.

New Zealand has some unusual wildlife. Many of the animals that are common across the world, such as mice, dogs and squirrels, do not live there naturally. However, many of these animals have now been brought to New Zealand by people.

Wetas are large crickets that took the place of mice. Just like mice, wetas live in burrows and eat almost anything they find lying around. However, there is something a weta can do that no mouse could manage. Wetas can hibernate in cold areas by squeezing into deep burrows. In the high mountains, some wetas are frozen solid in their winter dens! In spring, the insects thaw out and are perfectly fine. The wetas have antifreeze that stops ice from damaging their bodies.

Do you know...?

Jerusalem crickets (below) are relatives of wetas that live in North America. This species has a rather rough mating ritual. The male attracts a female by drumming his legs in his burrow. When his mate arrives, the pair make clicks with their jaws and begin to bite each other. After mating, the female often eats the male.

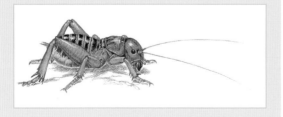

Why are mole crickets so noisy?

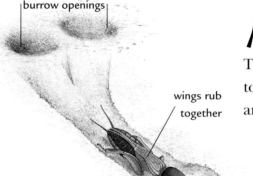

burrow openings

wings rub together

A European mole cricket in its burrow.

Do you know...?

Mole crickets spend much of their time under the ground. They tend to burrow in damp soil. During dry spells, when the soil dries out, the crickets head to deeper areas. The crickets dig with wide forelegs.

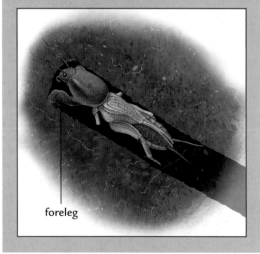

foreleg

Mole crickets are burrowing insects. They dig through the soil to find food, such as roots and insect grubs. Mole crickets have shorter feelers than other crickets because there is no room for them in tight burrows. Mole crickets are one of the noisiest insects in the world. The male calls to attract mates. These calls can be heard hundreds of metres away – not bad for an insect only 3 centimetres long! The crickets rub their forewings together to make high-pitched clicks. Their burrows make the calls louder. Each burrow has two rounded openings that form a 'Y' shape. The openings work like horns to send the calls out into the air.

Do crickets hear with their knees?

antenna

A European grasshopper has ears on its chest.

ear opening

Many insects make a lot of noises, but few are louder than grasshoppers and crickets. They sing by rubbing their wings or legs together to make clicking noises. But how do they hear their songs? A close look at a cricket's head will show you some eyes and a pair of sensors called antennae. But where are their ears? You are looking in the wrong place. Crickets have ears on the lower section of the leg, just below the 'knee' joint. Grasshoppers have ears on the chest area, between the front and middle legs. An insect's ear works in a similar way to your ear. It has an eardrum that wobbles back and forth when sound waves hit it. Sensors around the eardrum pick up these wobbles and send information to the brain.

Do you know...?

Pygmy grasshoppers (right) are less than 2 centimetres long. Some are just 8 millimetres in length, making them the smallest grasshopper of all. Most of the pygmies live on the ground. They are grey and brown, which helps them to stay hidden among fallen leaves.

Why do locusts form swarms?

A swarm of locusts is one of the largest and most destructive natural events on Earth. One swarm can contain 50 billion locusts (large grasshoppers). A swarm that size weighs about 80,000 tonnes – the same as 600 blue whales!

Swarms are not very common, but when they do occur, the insects eat all the plants they can find. Locust swarms have caused famines (times of starvation) because they eat all the food in a country.

Most of the time, locusts live alone like other grasshoppers. But if they are crowded together, the insects change into a swarming form. This form flies off in huge groups in search of less crowded places to live. The giant cloud of insects can block out the Sun.

An adult locust climbs a brightly coloured flower.

Do you know...?

Monkey grasshoppers are small, shiny insects that live in rainforests. They have a narrow body with a larger head than other grasshoppers. Their long faces and large eyes remind some people of a monkey. Monkey grasshoppers feed on animal poo and leaves.

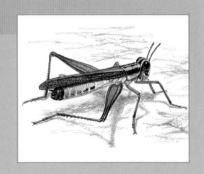

CHAPTER 2
FLIES

How many wings does a fly have?

Do you know...?

Some types of crane fly have hardly any wings at all. Snow flies live in the snow on the high slopes of mountains. They cannot fly, but flap their tiny wings to make space under the snow. The blanket of snow stops the flies from freezing. When it warms up a little, they climb out of the snow to look for food.

Not all insects have wings. Of those that do, most have two pairs, making a total of four. In some cases, insects only use one set of wings to fly – usually the front pair. A group of insects called the dipterans do just that. A dipteran is more commonly known as a fly. The front wings of a fly are long and narrow, which allows flies to be some of the most acrobatic fliers in the insect world. The fly's back wings look completely different. They are short rods with club-shaped tips. The rods are known as halteres. They sway around as the fly moves. The halteres' movements are sent to the brain, so the insect always knows which way up it is and how its body is moving.

Crane flies have long halteres that are easily visible behind the wings.

Which is the most dangerous insect in the world?

Although stinging wasps, killer bees and horseflies might give more painful stings and bites, the most dangerous insects are mosquitoes. Mosquitoes are little flies; their name means just that in Spanish.

A female mosquito sucks blood.

Female mosquitoes suck the blood of animals. They use this rich food to make their eggs. The flies pierce the skin with a sharp, needle-like mouth and inject a little saliva to stop the blood from clotting. The saliva contains tiny micro-organisms and viruses that cause diseases. Mosquito bites can spread illnesses such as malaria, yellow fever and West Nile virus. Malaria alone kills 1.5 million people each year, making it one of the world's most dangerous diseases.

Do you know...?

Mosquitoes lay their eggs in water. The eggs hatch into babies called larvae. These look a little like tiny caterpillars and feed on water plants. They breathe through a trumpet-shaped tube at the end of the body. The larvae poke it through the water's surface.

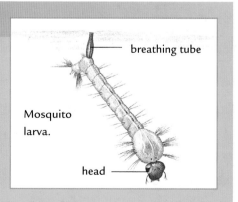

breathing tube

Mosquito larva.

head

Which fly can make you blind?

Black flies are chunky insects that spend their early lives in rivers. The young insects, known as larvae, stick themselves to stones with a sucker. That stops them being washed away while they sieve food from the water with brush-shaped mouthparts.

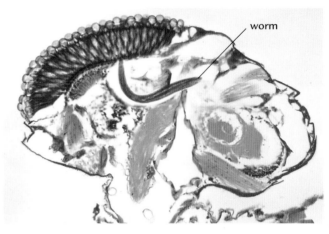

worm

An X-ray shows a worm from a black fly inside a brain.

The adults live above the surface. The males feed on pollen. Females suck the blood of larger animals, including people. Black flies in Africa and South America infect people with tiny worms. The worms grow under the skin, making itchy lumps. Large worms release smaller ones into the blood. These travel to the brain and attack the nerves that run to the eyes. That makes sufferers go blind so the disease is called river blindness. When a black fly bites a sufferer, it sucks some fresh worms up with blood, and passes them on to a new victim.

Do you know...?

Black flies are a type of midge. Most midges (below) do not bite. Some midge larvae live in tubes at the bottoms of muddy pools. They are bright red and named bloodworms.

male

female

female

A male love bug
courts two females.

What is a love bug?

March flies are large, hairy insects. One species, called the hawthorn fly, is often seen in March and April. But March flies have another name – the love bug. These flies get this name because they are often seen in breeding pairs. Breeding takes place in spring, when the flies form swarms in sunny spots in woodlands and gardens. The swarms are made up of male March flies. They are waiting for females to fly past. The largest and strongest flies hover in the lower part of the swarm. That is the best place to grab a passing female.

Do you know...?

Male march flies have huge eyes. They cover the whole of the tops of their heads, while a female's eyes (right) are on the sides. The male's larger eyes are built to detect females while flying along.

Do soldier flies fight a lot?

With a name like soldier fly, you might expect these insects to be fighting all the time. However, soldier flies are not particularly tough – they feed on flowers! The flies get their name from the bright colours on their abdomens. The abdomen is the rear section of an

Soldier flies like sunny areas.

Do you know...?

Most soldier fly larvae (young) eat dead plant material and dung that gets mixed into the soil. Some spend their early life in water. Soldier fly larvae have unusually rough skin. That is because it is covered in a chalky substance. That helps to waterproof the larva's skin, so it does not dry out. It also provides a barrier against tiny, attacking wasps, which try to inject their eggs inside the larva's body.

insect's body. The bright abdomens reminded the naturalists who first described the insects of the tunics worn by soldiers. Today, soldiers wear dull, camouflaged outfits. But in the past, they wore bright colours so they could easily see who was on their side during battles.

Most soldier flies have yellow stripes, while other species are bright green.

Why do only female horseflies drink blood?

Horseflies get their name because they are often seen around stables and in paddocks where horses are feeding. Horseflies suck the blood of horses, but they are not fussy and will bite people, too. Horseflies are large flies – about 2.5 centimetres long – and they give a painful bite! Horseflies and their close relatives, the deerflies, suck the blood of any large animal. However, only the females bite. The males only suck

A three-spot horsefly.

nectar from flowers. The females do that too, but they also need some richer food to make eggs. Each female will have at least one meal of blood after mating, most have more.

Do you know...?

The blinder deerfly (right) lives in Europe. It gets its name from the very unpleasant habit of biting the eyelids of deer and other victims! It is not surprising that the poor deer's eyelids swell up so much that it can barely see. The swelling is only temporary, but it must hurt. Blinder deerflies sometimes attack people, too, although only rarely.

How does a robber fly grab prey in mid-air?

Robber flies are large, hairy hunters that prey on other flying insects. They look scary but they are harmless to humans. But they are anything but harmless to gnats, midges and other smaller insects. Robber flies swoop through the air, grabbing these animals in mid-air.

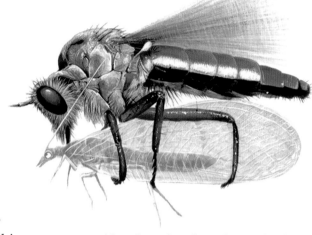

A robber fly grabs a lacewing. Its back legs work like pincers to hold on to prey.

Do you know...?

Some male robber flies go to great lengths to find a mate. A North American species lifts his mate's front legs up and down as if shaking hands, while others perform intricate dances, flashing coloured patches on their legs.

A robber fly has to be an excellent flier to catch prey. It uses its long, hairy legs to snatch victims. The front pair hang down in front of the fly as it comes into attack. The leg bristles help the fly to grip on to prey. The hind legs then bend around its prey to form a basket that nothing can escape from. Bristles on the face protect the fly's mouth from struggling prey, as it sticks a spike-shaped mouthpart into its victim's neck. The robber fly then sucks out the insides.

How do bee fly larvae feed?

A hovering bee fly uses its long tube-shaped mouth to drink nectar.

With their hairy, rounded bodies, bee flies look a lot like bumblebees. Like bees, they feed on the nectar in flowers. However, this insect has just two wings – bees and wasps have four – and that makes them a type of fly. Despite looking similar, bee flies lead very different lives to bees. Their young, or larvae, feed on the babies of other insects. After mating, a female finds the burrows of bees or beetles and lays her eggs nearby. Once the eggs hatch, the bee fly larvae crawl into the burrow and feast on the eggs and baby insects inside.

Do you know...?

Some female bee flies are precision bombers with their eggs. They hover 2 or 3 centimetres above the entrance to a beetle burrow and fire their eggs from mid-air. They rarely miss.

Tiger beetles are targeted by bee flies.

Why do midges fly around your head?

A swarm of midges.

Do you know...?

Very few insects can live in seawater, but some midges can. The females never grow legs or wings and live in cracks in the rocks on the shore. The males can swim, fly and walk on water to look for mates.

Have you ever been in the countryside in the summer and found yourself surrounded by a cloud of tiny insects? These are midges, and despite what people think, most of them do not bite. The midges are crowding together in an attempt to find a mate. The swarm, as the crowd is termed, is full of males. Swarms gather above tall objects. They can be seen above gateposts and streetlights, as well as people. The males jostle for the best position in the swarm so they can catch any females that fly past. The midges are in a hurry – they only live for a few days.

Why do dance flies dance?

A male dance fly kills another fly
to give as a present to its mate.

Dance flies are fierce little hunters that live in most parts of the world. They are expert fliers and are named after the complicated way the males attract female mates. If a male just flew over to a female, she might mistake him for prey. So the male doesn't take any chances. He first catches some prey, such as small gnat, and wraps it up in silk. With this wedding present slung below him, the male joins a crowd, or swarm, of other males. When a female arrives, he gives her the gift in mid-air. Then the male climbs on to the female's back to mate. The mates resemble a pair of dancers gliding across the dance floor.

Do you know...?

Some male dance flies do not bother catching a meal for their mates. Instead, they try to trick females by wrapping up a bundle of fluff from a plant. Others eat the insides of their prey and then offer the dry, empty remains to a female. Most females are not fooled by this behaviour. They might let the males mate with them, but not for very long. The females give much more time to the males that give them more tasty treats.

Hover flies feed on flowers, but what do their young live on?

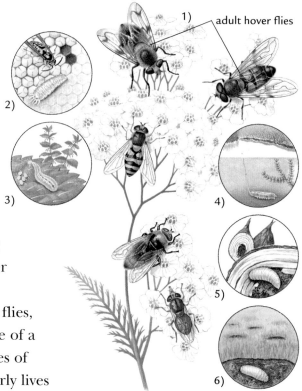

1) adult hover flies

Most hover fly adults (1) eat flower pollen and nectar. Some live in bees' nests (2); others prey on aphids (3); a rat-tailed maggot lives in water (4); bulb fly larvae on a bulb (5) and one species lays its eggs in cowpats (6).

People are often spooked by hover flies because they think the insects are wasps. That is what the fly wants them to think. Their black and yellow stripes are a disguise to fool people into thinking they are stinging insects. In fact, adult hover flies are harmless.

However, young hover flies, known as larvae, are more of a nuisance. Different species of hover flies spend their early lives in a range of habitats. Rat-tailed maggots are one species that live in water. The larvae 'snorkel' through a long tube at their rear end. Bulb flies lay their eggs in flower bulbs and onions. The larvae eat the bulb from the inside out, making it go brown and mushy. The flies are a pest for gardeners, florists and farmers.

Do you know...?

Even when caught by a spider, a hover fly produces a buzzing sound. Even though few escape, they still hope to convince their attackers that they are dangerous, stinging wasps.

How do stalk-eyed flies decide which is the stronger?

Stalk-eyed flies live in rainforests in Africa and Asia. They are among the weirdest-looking insects in the world. As their name suggests, the eyes of these tiny flies are on long stalks that stick out from the sides of their heads. On some males, both stalks together can be almost as wide as the length of the body. The stalks are so long that the flies can only just wipe them clean with the tips of their forelegs.

A pair of male stalk-eyed flies size each other up.

eye

Stalk-eyed flies can still see with their eyes so far apart. But they feed on sweet liquids, such as sap and honeydew, so they do not need to have great vision to find food. Instead, the flies use their eyes as a symbol of their strength. When two males are competing for mates, they stand head-to-head. The fly with the longest stalks wins the female.

Do you know...?

Stilt-legged flies (right) live in the rainforests of South America. They stalk around on their long legs and hunt for midges that live in rotting wood. The flies fight over the best hunting sites by rearing up on their back legs and staring at each other in an insect face-off.

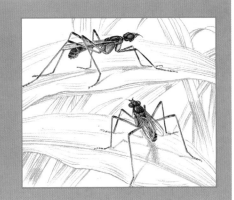

Why are fruit flies used to study genes?

Genes are the instructions needed to make a living organism. One small insect has helped scientists understand genes more than any other animal – the little fruit fly, called *Drosophila*. Every cell in a body contains a full set of genes, which are held in structures called chromosomes. Certain cells in *Drosophila* flies have huge

Drosophila fruit flies feed on rotting fruit.

chromosomes that are easy to study under a microscope. Scientists can also breed fruit flies very quickly, so they can easily find out how changes to certain genes will affect the way a body grows.

Do you know...?

Not all fruit flies are as useful as *Drosophila*. Most are serious pests because they damage fruit crops. The walnut husk fly (right) is one such pest. It lays its eggs inside the husk, or shell, of walnuts. The nut inside is not damaged, but the shell is covered in nasty slime.

How are snail flies used to control pests?

Do you know...?

One of the most damaging insect pests is the medfly (below). This fruit fly lives naturally in southern Europe but has now spread to attack fruits across the world. Scientists use biology to control the flies. They set traps that release the scent of male flies. Thousands of females arrive and are killed.

Snails and slugs do a lot of damage to gardens and farm crops across the world. There are chemicals, called pesticides, that kill the animals. But the pesticides can also attack the other beasties in the area that are good for the environment. So scientists use an insect to target pesty snails and slugs. Snail flies, also named marsh flies, lay their eggs on the backs of snails and slugs. The young flies, or larvae, feed on the bodies of the snails. Some larvae inject poison into the snail and then eat the body. Other larvae keep their host snails alive. The snail dies when the insect is big enough to become an adult. Farmers use snail flies to tackle snail pests.

An adult snail fly looks for a snail to lay its eggs on.

How do bot fly larvae get under your skin?

Bot flies are very unpleasant flies. They do not sting or bite people. But they do something even worse – they lay their eggs under your skin. Only American flies called skin bots target people. Most bot flies use large animals, like cattle and deer, as hosts for their larvae. Bot fly adults do not eat. Instead, they spend all of their time looking for mates and then a host for their eggs. Most lay their eggs on the hairs of a host's leg. When the young insects, called larvae, hatch, they burrow into the skin and gorge themselves on flesh. As they grow, the larvae form bulges. Other bot flies fire eggs into a host's nose.

Do you know...?

A parasite is a creature that lives on or inside the body of another animal, or host. Adult parasite flies feed on nectar, but they lay their eggs on or inside other insects, such as caterpillars (below). Parasite fly larvae eventually kill their hosts.

adult

A bot fly larva grows under the skin with a little air tube poking out.

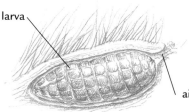

larva

air tube

How do dung flies kill their prey?

Flies love dung, the droppings of large animals, such as cattle and deer. The dung is full of half-eaten food and it makes a perfect place for young, or larvae, to grow. Many flies lay their eggs in dung, including dung flies themselves. However, adult dung flies also use cowpats as bait for

Dung flies hunt on cowpats.

their prey. The dung fly lurks out of sight beside the poo waiting for a victim to arrive. Then the dung fly leaps on its prey's back and stabs it in the back of the neck with a pointed mouthpart bristling with knife-like points. That cut slashes through the prey's main nerve, killing it immediately. The dung fly then sucks out the juicy insides through the hole in the neck.

Do you know...?

Dung flies lay their eggs in cowpats, and the competition for mates is fierce. The males wait at cowpats for a female to arrive. Often one female is swamped by several males. As the males scramble to beat their rivals, the poor female fly is pushed into the soft dung – and may drown!

What do houseflies use to taste their food?

A housefly samples its food with its feet!

Houseflies are among the most widespread animals on Earth. They live alongside people, surviving on the waste we leave behind. Adult houseflies eat a wide range of food, and their young, known as maggots, thrive in dung and rotting food. Houseflies buzz around looking for something to eat and a place to lay their eggs. They have taste sensors on their feet, so the fly can decide whether something is tasty food or not just by landing on it!

Do you know...?

As the name suggests, stable flies often live close to horses. Stable flies look very similar to their close relatives, the houseflies, but stable flies give a nasty bite. They often bite without warning, most commonly on the ankles. However, the bites are completely harmless.

A housefly has a bite to eat.

Are houseflies dangerous?

Houseflies eat liquid food, using a spongy mouth tube to mop it up. The flies suck up the juices that ooze from rotting waste. They can also turn solid food into a liquid by squirting the contents of their stomach on to it. The stomach juices digest the food, making it into a goo that the fly can suck up. This feeding behaviour makes the housefly a dangerous pest. The stomach juices contain bacteria and other micro-organisms that cause diseases. When these get on to food that people eat, they can become ill. Houseflies spread common diseases, such as diarrhoea and stomach worms, as well as deadly ones, such as dysentery, cholera and typhoid.

Do you know...?

Tsetse flies (pronounced tetsee, below) are flies that live in Africa. They suck blood from animals, including people, and spread a deadly disease called sleeping sickness. The disease can puts sufferers into a coma.

What makes cattle gad about?

Cattle are targets for flesh-eating warble flies.

Have you heard the phrase 'gadding about'? People use it to describe someone who is always dashing around. The phrase comes from the behaviour of a herd of cattle. Most of the time, cattle are quiet animals that rarely break into a run. However, cattle start gadding when they hear the buzz of warble flies, a type of bot fly, that are coming to attack the cows. They trot around in circles, making small jumps, as they try to stop flies from landing on them and laying eggs.

Maggots might be good for your health.

Do maggots help wounds heal?

A young insect is called a larva. The larvae of certain flies, such as houseflies and bluebottles, are known as maggots. People don't like to see maggots because they are found in places that are very dirty. However, they do have their uses. Maggots make excellent bait for anglers. And for centuries, maggots have been used to help bad wounds to heal. The maggots of blow flies eat flesh, and they clean all the dead skin around a wound and stop it from getting infected. Even today, maggots reared in clean conditions are used for this purpose.

A blow fly's maggots are used to clean cuts.

Do you know...?

Jackal flies get their name because they steal food, just like real jackals. The tiny flies creep up on other hunting insects and suck up the blood that drips from prey.

33

Flesh flies lay eggs on meat.

How do termites and flesh flies live together?

Adult flesh flies feed on flowers, but their young eat meat. Most types eat the remains of dead animals, but some have close associations with other insects. One species in South Africa lays its eggs in the nests of termites. Normally, soldier termites throw out any invaders to the nest. But when the larvae (young insects) hatch out they are raised by the termites. The termites feed the growing fly larvae and keep them safe in the nest. In return, the larvae produce fatty liquids that the termites eat.

Are screwworms insects?

Screwworms are the maggots of a type of blow fly that lives in North America. In that part of the world, they are a dangerous threat to farm animals.

Most types of blow fly lay their eggs on flesh. Female screwworm flies lay their eggs around the umbilical cords of newborn lambs, foals and calves. The umbilical cord is the tube that connects the newborn to its mother. Once they hatch, the screwworms tunnel into the baby's belly button and create a dangerous wound that can kill.

Screwworms are the young of certain blow flies.

Screwworms attack lambs.

Do you know...?

The Congo floor maggot is the young of a blow fly from Central Africa. It sucks human blood, especially when people are sleeping on the floor. This is one of the few insects that preys only on people. However, the maggots cannot climb, so sleeping in a bed is safe.

CHAPTER 3
BUGS

Isn't 'bug' just another word for 'insect'?

Some people call all the creepy-crawlies they see bugs. To them, beetles, butterflies, spiders, worms and woodlice are just another type of bug. Biologists, the people that study plants and animals, use the word bug, too. But they use it only as the name of a certain group of insects. There are nearly 100,000 types of these bugs. Bugs that you might have heard of include

A cicada is a type of bug.

cicadas, bedbugs, pondskaters and greenfly. In general, bugs feed on liquid food. They have sharp, pointed mouthparts. Most bugs also have four wings. The front half of the forewings often have a scaly covering.

Do you know...?

A bug's mouthparts form a pointed hollow tube. The tube is used to squirt saliva (spit) and suck up food. It is formed from four separate parts that are fused into a pipe with two hollow sections. The pipe is flexible, so the bug can bend it to reach food.

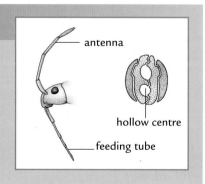

antenna

hollow centre

feeding tube

37

Why don't pondskaters sink?

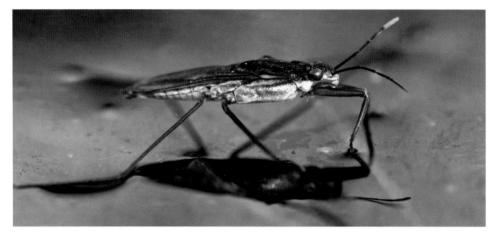

A pondskater, or water strider, walks across the surface of water.

Adult pondskaters don't live in water, they live on top of it. They walk across the surface of calm pools. Pondskaters stand on their middle and back legs – the front pair are used to catch prey. The legs are covered in hairs that help them to float. The insects can stand on the water's surface because it clings together, making something called surface tension. The pondskaters are only light, so their legs do not push down hard enough to break through the surface.

Do you know...?

Relatives of pondskaters are some of the very few insects to live in the sea. Sea striders walk on the surface of warm oceans and they are often hundreds of miles from land. Females lay their eggs on a floating bird's feather or a bit of wood.

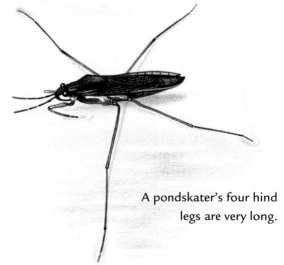

A pondskater's four hind legs are very long.

How does a water cricket's spit help it to slide across water?

A water cricket is also known as a ripple bug.

Water crickets are not related to grasshoppers or other crickets. Instead, they are a type of bug that hunts on the surface of streams and ponds. The water cricket searches for insects that have fallen into the water. Water crickets have hairy feet, which lets them push against the water, so the insects can walk and run on the surface, or skate along.

However, if a water cricket needs to move at top speed it has a special trick. The insect spits a drop of saliva onto the water in front of it. The spit reduces the surface tension of the water in front of the cricket. It is only a tiny amount of saliva, but water floods into this area and that is enough to drag the cricket with it. This makes the cricket scoot across the water.

Do you know...?

Water crickets and pondskaters prey on drowning insects that have fallen into water. They find these prey by picking up the ripples the insects make as they struggle to swim. The bugs grab prey with their front legs and suck the juicy insides out through their pointed mouthparts.

How do plant bug nymphs hold on in emergencies?

Most plant bugs suck juice from leaves and fruits.

A young bug is called a nymph. The nymphs of some plant bugs have a very strange way of clinging onto a leaf if an attacker tries to pull them off. The little bugs push the bottom end of their intestines (gut tubes) out of their bottoms. The intestines stick to the leaf and make it hard for the attacker to pick up the nymph.

Do you know...?

Some bugs live in the webs of spiders. The bugs stay quiet at night when the spider is awake but during the day they creep around the web, feeding on flies and other insects that have fallen victim to the spider.

A pair of plant bugs.

How does a water scorpion go snorkelling?

Despite their name, water scorpions are not a type of scorpion at all. They are, in fact, a type of bug. Scorpions have powerful pincers, and water scorpions are named after their large pincer-like forelegs that they use to catch prey in the water. Water scorpions also have long tails that stick out behind the body and look a bit like a scorpion's tail. Unlike a scorpion, the insect does not use its tail as a stinger. Instead, the tail is really a tube that the water scorpion uses as a snorkel. A water scorpion hangs upside down with its snorkel poking out through the surface.

_____ breathing tube

A water scorpion's tail is actually a breathing tube.

A real scorpion.

Do you know...?

The giant water bug is another insect that hunt in water. At 6 centimetres long it is the largest of all bugs. The bugs paddle with their hind legs, which are covered in thick hairs. In America, giant water bugs are known as toe biters because they give painful nips.

How do you know if you have bedbugs?

Do you know...?

Bedbugs do not just live in beds. They are also found in birds' nests and bat caves. In the wild, bedbugs often have to wait for a meal. They can survive without eating for more than a year.

Don't let the bedbugs bite! Everyone has heard that fun phrase, but do you ever get bitten? Modern houses are now very clean, so bedbugs are rare. But just 70 years ago, about four million people in London alone were being attacked by these little blood-suckers every night.

Bed bugs spend the day hidden in nooks and crannies. They come out at night – or when you turn the lights off – and look for a warm body to suck blood from. A bedbug bite is a small, dry swelling that can be itchy. Houses with bedbugs are treated with chemicals to kill them all.

Bedbugs crawl through a person's skin hairs.

42

How did the toad bug get its name?

Toad bugs are little insects that live in warm parts of the world. They are most often seen among rotting leaves around small forest pools. This type of habitat is also home to toads and frogs. Sometimes toad bugs are mistaken for toads. They are flat and round insects with bumpy skin that looks like the warts of a toad. Also like a toad, toad bugs have bulging eyes, and the bugs have only very short antennae (feelers), which makes it harder to spot that they are insects. However, the most confusing thing is that toad bugs hop instead of walk. When they are not moving, the bugs look like pebbles.

A toad bug looks a bit like a toad.

bump

bulging eyes

Do you know...?

Most shore bugs are tiny insects that live in a similar habitat to toad bugs, where they might end up as a toad bug's lunch. They are also found on seashores and along the banks of river mouths. The marine bug is a shore bug that lives on rocky shores in western Europe. It has tiny wings so it can squeeze into cracks and under rocks. At 3 millimetres long, it is one of the smallest bugs.

A real toad has warty skin.

How do water boatmen carry their air supply under water?

Water boatmen are also known as backswimmers because they hang upside down from the surface of the water. They cling on to the water with claws on their front and middle legs. The insect uses its back legs as oars and rows along on its back. The back legs are fringed with hairs to push against the water. There are hairs on the boatman's belly that trap tiny bubbles of air when the insect dives under water. Larger water boatman also carry air under their wings. The insect breathes from these air bubbles when it is under water.

A water boatman seen from above.

Do you know...?

A water boatman's eyes are on the top of its head so when it is swimming the eyes look down. Most boatmen scan the water below and dive down to spear prey with their pointed mouthparts. Other types creep underneath prey on the surface and grab them from below.

A swimming water boatman looks like a person rowing a boat upside down.

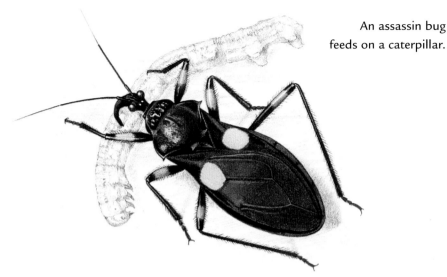

An assassin bug feeds on a caterpillar.

How does an assassin bug kill?

Assassin bugs are the hitmen of the insect world. Many are highly camouflaged, so they can sit and wait for prey to come past and then kill it silently and swiftly. An assassin bug grabs its prey with powerful front legs. The insect then thrusts its sturdy, pointed mouthparts into a victim's body. The bug pumps saliva into its prey, which turns the insides into a fleshy soup. The assassin can now suck up the goo, leaving an empty husk.

Do you know...?

Several types of assassin bug do not kill prey but suck the blood of large animals, including people. They drink so much blood that they are too heavy to fly away afterwards. The bugs that live in Central and South America sometimes spread a dangerous illness called Chaga's disease. Chaga's disease attacks the heart and makes sufferers die young.

Damsel bugs kill prey in a similar way to assassin bugs.

How do resin bugs attract prey?

A wheel bug is a type of assassin bug with a cog-shaped back.

Do you know...?

Very few insects take care of their young. Assassin bugs do, though. Insect eggs are attacked by tiny wasps, so after mating (below), some male assassin bugs stand guard over their eggs. They try to spear any wasps that come close.

Assassin bugs are cunning killers that employ many tools and weapons. Wheel bugs are equipped with a rounded, spiked shield on their backs so they can take on prey that are even larger than themselves.

Resin bugs use bait to lure prey within their reach. The bugs coat their forelegs with resin – a sticky liquid that oozes from tree bark. The resin is collected by certain bees and termites to make their nests. The resin bug stands with its resin-coated legs raised up. When bees and termites come to collect the resin, the killer bug lunges forwards with its spear-like mouth!

Why do milkweed bugs have red wings?

Milkweed bugs are a type of seed bug. Most seed bugs are drab-coloured insects that rummage through fallen leaves for seeds. However, milkweed bugs have patches of bright red on their backs. That colour is a warning message to other insects that says, "Don't eat me!"

Milkweed bugs feed on milkweed – as their name suggests. They suck the juices from the plant. The juices contain a mixture of poisonous chemicals. The bugs are not affected by the poisons. Instead, they store the poison inside their bodies, which makes the bugs themselves poisonous. Eating a milkweed bug won't kill, but it will make a bird or another hunter very sick. They soon learn to avoid eating the red insects.

A milkweed bug rests on a milkweed pod.

Do you know...?

Fire bugs (below) are another type of red bug. They live in the United States and are often seen in spring.

47

What are stainers?

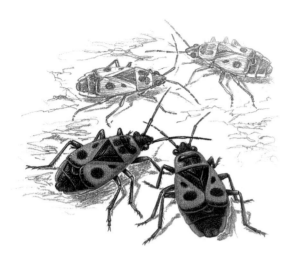

Stainers are also known as fire bugs, or simply red bugs.

Stainers are bugs with very long mouthparts, which they use for piercing seeds and fruits. Most stainers are bright red, but that is not the reason for their name. The name comes from the damage the bugs cause to cotton and kapok plants. These plants are grown around the world as a source of fibres, which are woven into material. The stainers attack the plant's seeds causing them to leak a thin liquid, called sap. It is this sap that stains the cotton and kapok fibres, making them useless.

Stainers feed on the seeds of cotton plants, which damages the white cotton fibres.

Why should you stay away from a leaf-footed bug?

Leaf-footed bugs get their name from their back legs, which are slightly flattened. The legs also have ribs running along them that look a little like the veins on a leaf. Many leaf-footed bugs have sharp spines running along the edges of the back legs. These spines make it harder to grab the bugs from

Leaf-footed bugs have flattened hind legs.

behind. However, the bugs have another way of keeping predators at bay. Glands – structures that release liquids – on the bug's chest area produce a nasty smell. If that is not enough to keep attackers away, then the bug squirts an equally horrible liquid from its bottom all over the threat.

Do you know...?

Shield bugs are named after the armour plate that runs from the head to the middle of the back. With their rounded bodies, some shield bugs are named tortoise bugs. Most types of shield bug suck the juice from leaves and stems. Many are crop pests.

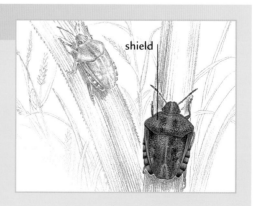

shield

Why are stink bugs so smelly?

A stink bug.

One of the largest families of bugs are called stink bugs. Like many similar families, these bugs have a protective shield on their necks. In fact, some are known as shield bugs, which makes them easily confused with another family, also known as shield bugs.

However, stink bugs have an obvious difference: they release horrible-smelling liquids from stink glands on their thoraxes. 'Thorax' is the scientific name for an insect's chest area. The smell of the glands is a warning to predators that the bug is not going to taste very nice. Stink bugs raise their bottoms into the air so the wind catches the whiff and spreads it to the surrounding area.

Do you know...?

Stink bug eggs grow darker as the baby bug, or nymph, grows inside. When it is ready to hatch, the nymph uses a T-shaped 'tooth' that bursts out of the egg.

A stink bug's head pokes out from under its armoured shield.

What is cuckoo spit?

Cuckoo spit is a frothy substance that appears on plants in spring. The froth is not made by cuckoos. The name comes from the fact that it appears at the same time of year as the first cuckoos can be heard in the countryside.

Cuckoo spit is actually made by insects called spittlebugs. It is the young bug, or nymph,

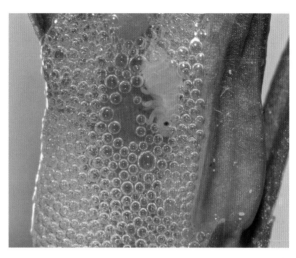

Philaenus spumarius or Meadow Spittlebugs get their name from the foam made by the spittlebug nymphs. They live their young lives in it.

that makes the froth. Once it hatches, the nymph sucks the liquid, called sap, out of a plant's stem. Sap is mainly water, and the nymph has to drink a lot of it to get all the goodness it needs to grow. The nymph gets rid of the extra water by peeing. It mixes the pee with a bubble liquid and whips it into a froth with its legs. The nymph hides inside the froth to avoid predators.

Adult spittlebugs can leap long distances.

Do you know...?

Spittlebugs are also known as froghoppers because the adults can make large leaps. They have long back legs, like a grasshopper, that allow them to do this.

How long does it take for a cicada to grow up?

Most insects start life looking very different to their parents. Caterpillars change into butterflies. Maggots become flies. Young bugs are called nymphs. Most nymphs make the change into adults after a few weeks. However, some species of cicadas wait years before becoming adults.

A winged adult cicada climbs out of the body of a wingless nymph.

Do you know...?

Cicadas (below) have powerful wing muscles. Some cicadas warm the rest of their bodies with the heat made by these muscles. That allows the insects to be active on cold days.

In that time, the nymphs live underground, sucking sap from the roots of trees. It takes them a long time to grow to full size on this watery diet. When it is time to make the change, the nymphs climb up the tree trunk, and adults burst out of the nymphs' skins.

A few species take 13 years to reach adulthood, while others wait for 17 years. In those years huge numbers of cicadas appear. The cicadas choose 13 and 17 years because those numbers make it very hard for predators to predict when the new adults will be arriving.

How do cicadas sing so loudly?

Cicadas are some of the noisiest insects. When many cicadas are singing together the sound can be deafening! Only male cicadas sing and they produce

buzzes or loud clicks. The cicadas make these noises with plates inside the abdomen (rear body section). Each plate is made of stiff material and is shaped into a curve. When a muscle pulls on the plate, it pops into a curve that bends the other way. That movement makes a click.

When the muscle relaxes, the plate clicks back into its original shape. The plates are clicked many times per second.

A cicada calls from a tree trunk.

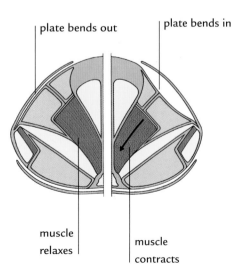

plate bends out   plate bends in

muscle relaxes   muscle contracts

How do treehoppers look after their young?

A treehopper.

Do you know...?

In Florida, treehoppers lay eggs in the bark of powderpuff plants (below). Before the eggs hatch, their mother cuts a spiral of bark away to make a feeding site for the young.

Treehoppers are plant bugs that suck the juices out of plant stems and branches. The bugs often live in large numbers, and although they try to stay out of sight it is sometimes impossible to avoid the attention of spiders and meat-eating insects. The largest crowds are formed by treehopper nymphs (young), which gather in one place to feed after hatching. This is the most dangerous time of their lives. In many species, the nymphs' mother stays with her young to protect them from attack. Even when they are still inside the eggs, the adult bug chases attackers away.

54

Are thorn bugs pretending to be thorns?

Thorn bugs are a type of treehopper. As you can see from the picture, the bugs have pointed covers over their bodies. All treehoppers have a similar armour plate. Some use theirs to pretend to be ants or bird droppings. However, thorn bugs are the shape of a thorn that might grow on a rose bush. But there is one big difference: thorn bugs are brightly coloured. Why do they pretend to be thorns if they are just going to show off with bright patterns? Experts think that thorn bugs are actually shaped the way they are to make it harder for predators to get them in their mouths.

Thorn bugs are easy to see.

Do you know...?

Leafhoppers (right) live a similar life to treehoppers but they do not have the same pointed armour. They are called leafhoppers because they have long back legs, which they use to make giant leaps, a bit like a grasshopper. Once in the air, leafhoppers open their wings and fly away.

long back leg

Why do ants keep herds of aphids?

An ant minds its herd of aphids.

Do you know...?

Aphids (below) are attacked by tiny wasps. They defend themselves by releasing a drop of glue onto their backs. That sticks the wasp to the aphid. Both will die, but the wasp will not hurt any more aphids.

Like many plant bugs, aphids feed on sap. Sap is a watery liquid that runs through plants. The bugs drink so much that they have to get rid of all the waste water. They do this by producing a liquid called honeydew. Honeydew also contains the waste sugar from the sap. That sugar makes honeydew taste sweet.

Many types of ant like to drink honeydew. It is not uncommon for one or two ants to keep a herd of aphids. The ants protect the aphids from attack, so they can continue to suck up the sap. When the ant feels hungry it 'milks' one of the aphids by gently stroking it. That makes the aphid produce a droplet of honeydew for its master.

Why do aphids give birth without mating?

Although they are only tiny, aphids have a very complicated life. The adults die in winter; only the eggs can survive the cold weather. The eggs hatch in spring and they are all females. Even after they become adults, none of them have wings. These females can have babies without needing to mate

Aphids are sometimes called green flies.

with a male. They simply give birth to another baby female. Like its mother, this aphid can reproduce without mating. This breeding system allows the aphids to increase in number very quickly and make the most of whatever food is out there. When food runs low, the aphids produce females with wings and then males with wings. The males and females mate to produce the eggs for the following year.

Do you know...?

Soldier aphids are giant nymphs (young bugs) that are not able to grow into adults. Instead it is their job to defend the other aphids from attack from ladybirds (right) or other threats. The soldier aphids use their pointed mouthparts as weapons to stab anything that gets too close.

Can scale insects move at all?

Scale insects once lived in just Africa and the Americas. However, today these unusual members of the bug family now live all over the world. They have been spread on plants that have been transported to new parts of the world.

Adult male scale insects never eat anything. They have no mouth at all.

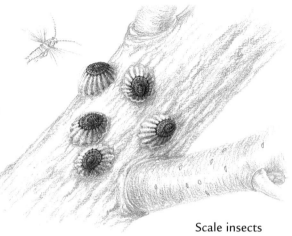

Scale insects on a branch.

Do you know...?

Mealybugs (below) are tiny insects that suck sap. They are usually pests. Females are always wingless, while males sometimes have wings. The name 'mealy' refers to the way the insects look like they are covered in flour, or meal.

All males do is look for mates, usually by fluttering from branch to branch. That is where the female scale insects are drinking sap. They stick their pointed mouthparts into the plant and suck out the juices. Once they are feeding, the females do not bother moving; their legs are so short, they cannot walk anyway. Staying in one place is a dangerous thing to do for such a small insect, so it grows a protective cover, or scale over the upper body.

CHAPTER 4
BEETLES

Where do beetles keep their wings?

Beetles spend a lot of their time crawling around on the ground or on plants. You might have seen some species going about their business, such as ladybirds with their smooth and shiny red backs. If you get too close, a beetle will probably fly away. But it looks like there are no wings on its back. How does it fly?

elytra

hind wing

Most flying insects have four wings in two pairs, but a beetle gets off the ground with just two. Because it spends a lot of time scrabbling through rough terrain, the beetle keeps its wings protected under hard wing cases, or elytra. The elytra are made from the insect's front wings, which grow thick and hard.

A beetle flies with its elytra raised.

Do you know...?

There are more than one million species of animal, probably many more. Insects are by far the largest group of animal, making 90 percent of the total. Beetles form the largest group of insects. One in every three insects is a type of beetle.

How do bombardier beetles burn attackers?

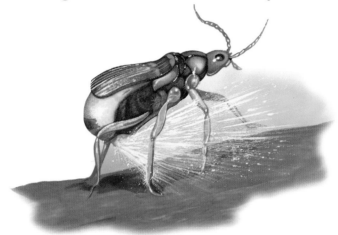

B ombardier beetles are ground-living insects that have an amazing defence system. When a bombardier beetle is attacked, it squirts a spray of acid at its enemies from the tip of its abdomen (rear end). The acid burns attackers, which must quickly wipe it off. The beetle can fire 20 times before running out of spray.

The spray is so powerful that it actually causes a tiny explosion as it is released. This explosion can be heard as a pop, and a puff of smoke comes out of the beetle's body. The beetle itself is safe because it makes two chemicals, which are harmless on their own. As the beetle fires, the two chemicals are mixed to form the explosive liquid.

A bombardier beetle can fire its spray of hot acid in any direction.

Do you know...?

Ground beetles (below) are mainly hunters. One type from Arizona doesn't catch its own food. Instead, it 'mugs' ants that are carrying prey back to the nest. The beetle tracks the ants by their scent and also raids their nests.

How do diving beetles breathe under water?

Diving beetles spend nearly all of their lives in water. As young, or larvae, the beetles are fierce hunters that prey on little fish, tadpoles and other insects with their powerful, fang-like mouthparts. The larvae breathe under water using gills. However, the adults breathe air through tubes positioned around their bodies.

Adult diving beetles paddle with their hairy back legs.

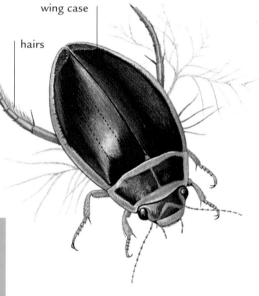

wing case

hairs

Do you know...?

Whirligig beetles are tiny water insects that live on the surfaces of ponds. They float well because of water-repelling hairs on their bodies. Whirligigs (below) get their name from the way they zip around the surface in circles and zigzags.

The beetle comes to the surface to breathe and it takes a supply of air under water with it. The beetle pokes its abdomen (rear body section) out of the water to allow bubbles of air to form under the wing cases.

Adult diving beetles make short flights to find new pools to live in. They are easily confused and often crash into glass or other shiny surfaces, thinking they are water.

Do tiger beetles have stripes?

Tiger beetles are most common in warm, dry parts of the world, such as deserts. They are good fliers, but the beetles spend most of their time hunting on the ground. They have long legs and can run very fast. But why are they named after tigers?

Tiger beetles use their long legs to lift them clear of the hot ground.

No tiger beetle has stripes, many are just black, while most have bright blobs of colour. A few species have yellow and black markings, but metallic blues and greens are more common. One of the reasons for the name of tiger beetles is the way they catch prey. Like their big-cat namesake, tiger beetles chase their prey and kill with with a crushing bite from large fangs.

Do you know...?

A male tiger beetle does not bother to woo a mate. He just climbs onto the back of any passing female. She will try to throw him off, but he holds on tight by fitting his large fangs into grooves, called sulci, on the side of the female's body.

A tiger beetle.

Do undertaker beetles bury bodies?

Undertaker beetles are attracted by the smell of dead bodies.

Undertaker beetles feed their young on the rotting flesh of dead animals. A male beetle finds a corpse (dead body) of a small animal, such as a mouse, bird or frog. He then produces a strong scent that attracts a female mate. The pair dig around the corpse so it is gradually lowered into the ground. As they dig, the beetles cut away fur or feathers. The beetles cover themselves and the corpse with soil to make a crypt. Inside, the female lays eggs all over the corpse.

Other carrion beetles feed on the bodies of dead animals.

Do you know...?

Some carrion beetles do not bury their corpse. Instead, they look for signs that another pair of beetles has done it and then dig down into the crypt. They fight the adult beetles already inside and kill any larvae in the nest before laying their own eggs in the rotting carrion.

Why do rove beetles have bright, flexible tails?

A rove beetle.

At first glance, rove beetles look like ants. They have narrow bodies and a flexible abdomen (rear end) like an ant. However, close up you can see that the beetle does not have an ant's tiny 'waist'.

Rove beetles curl their abdomens to point upwards, which gives them the nickname cock-tail beetles. The tail is often brightly coloured, making it easy to see. The tail is held up as a warning to other animals. Rove beetles cannot sting but their abdomen is armed with stink glands that squirt nasty-smelling liquids.

Do you know...?

Some types of rove beetle live in ants' nests (below), which are quite hostile places. The beetles survive with tough armour against the stings, while others blast any attacking ants with knock-out spray. Some ants allow the beetles to stay because they eat rubbish and also because they offer the ants a tasty, sweet liquid.

How do fireflies produce light?

As is often the case with insects with interesting names, fireflies are not flies. They are also known as lightning bugs, but they are not a type of bug either. Instead, fireflies are a type of beetle.

Both male and female fireflies produce light in segments of their abdomens (rear ends). The light is made when two chemicals are mixed together. The reaction produces yellow–green light.

Only male fireflies can fly. They fly around making a series of flashes. Each species uses a certain sequence of flashes. When a female perching on a branch sees the correct sequence, she turns on her lights as a beacon for the male to aim for.

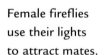

Female fireflies use their lights to attract mates.

A male firefly.

Do you know...?

Glowworms are not worms, but beetles. Like many beetles, these insects start life as worm-like grubs. The adult males look like small soldier beetles, but the females never grow out of their grub bodies. Both the young and the females produce light as they crawl around on the ground.

Why do chequered beetle larvae hitch rides on passing bees?

Chequered beetles are little insects that live mainly in the south-west of the United States. The adults eat the nectar and pollen of flowers, and females lay their eggs one by one on the blooms. After hatching, the larva stays on the flower, waiting for a bee or a wasp to arrive. The larva jumps onto the visiting insect and stays on board until it reaches its ride's nest. The beetle larva then dismounts and begins to feed on the eggs and larvae of its bee or wasp hosts.

An adult chequered beetle.

This bumblebee might have a passenger.

Do you know...?

Female chequered beetles do not make a fuss about mating. A male usually waits until his chosen mate is about to start a meal. Only then does he fly down and climb on to her back. The female keeps on eating during mating. She will not stop feeding even when several males are on her back fighting over her.

How can a click beetle disappear into thin air?

Click beetles often land on their backs after a click, but they eventually right themselves.

peg in notch

Click beetles are named after the way they escape from danger. If the beetle is knocked onto its back by a predator, it arches its back so a peg on its underside slots into a notch.

Do you know...?

The larvae, or young, of click beetles are called wireworms. Wireworms have very short legs and are covered in a tough skin. They survive by burrowing like a worm through soil. They eat the roots of plants and are a major pest for farmers. They attack crops such as cotton, wheat, corn, and damage flower bulbs.

A strong muscle then forces the peg out of the notch very quickly, producing a loud click. The beetle's body springs out of the arch shape. The head and tail sections are pushed on to the ground and that launches the body into the air.

The beetle is thrown up 30 centimetres – about 10 times its own length. The forces needed to do that to a human body would easily kill a person. It all happens so fast that the beetle appears to disappear before landing safely nearby.

Why do jewel beetles sparkle and shine?

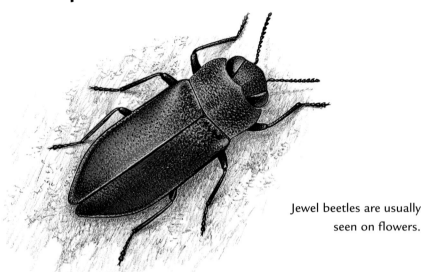

Jewel beetles are usually seen on flowers.

The people of some South American tribes use the wing cases of jewel beetles to make pieces of jewellery. The insects' shiny greens and blues are not made by natural dyes, or pigments. Instead, the sparkles are created by the different ways light reflects off the surface. Some light bounces off the very top layer of the wing case, while other rays pass through and reflect off structures lower down. The different reflected rays mix together to make a shimmering pattern of colours.

Do you know...?

Soldier beetles are named after their red and black colouring, which looks like the uniform of a European soldier from 200 years ago. Adult soldier beetles (right) are peaceful creatures, feeding on nectar and pollen. The bold colouring is a warning to birds and other predators that soldier beetles do not taste nice.

How did the deathwatch beetle get its name?

A deathwatch beetle spends its early life in wood.

Few insects have a name as interesting as the deathwatch beetle. These small beetles are a dangerous pest because their larvae (young) eat wood. The larvae leave a network of tunnels inside that makes the wood very weak. If the insects get into the timbers holding up a house, the beetles can actually make it fall down.

The name comes from the way the beetles tap out messages while feeding in wood. The noises are very quiet, and according to tradition they are heard when people wait in silence around the bed of a person about to die. The beetles' taps were thought to be the ticks of a clock counting down to the end of the person's life.

Do you know...?

In the wild, carpet beetles survive by eating the hairs of dead animals. Wool is sheep hair and woollen carpets provide an almost unending supply of food for the tiny beetles and their larvae. The beetles (right) now live in all parts of the world, eating carpets.

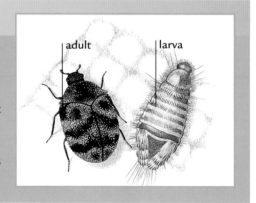

adult   larva

How did the ladybird get its name?

A ladybird feasts on aphids, or greenflies, which are common garden pests.

Ladybirds are very familiar beetles. In North America, the same beetles are known as ladybugs. Ladybirds eat small insects such as aphids, mealybugs and scale insects, which suck sap from plants. These sap-suckers are pests that attack fruit crops and flowers. Before the invention of chemical sprays that kill the pests, the best a farmer could hope for was that ladybirds might eat the harmful insects. When the ladybirds came to the rescue, European farmers gave thanks to Our Lady (the Virgin Mary) and named the beetles after her.

Do you know...?

Ladybird larvae (young, right) have a rather nasty way of shooing away predators. They leak blood from their bottoms. The blood smells bad and tastes even worse, so most predators choose to eat something else.

Do all ladybirds have spots?

A seven-spot ladybird,
or Coccinella 7-punctata.

Do you know...?

The male of an Australian species of ladybird chooses a mate when she is still a pupa – the stage when a larva is changing into an adult. The male can tell if a pupa is female by its taste. He then waits for her to hatch into an adult and they mate straight away.

Not all ladybirds are red. Many are orange or yellow, while some have reversed their colouring so they are black with bright spots. Some species have markings that cannot really be described as spots, but those are rare. Most ladybirds are spotted, and many species are named after the number of spots they have. The species' scientific names also include a number to show how many spots it has. For example, the two-spotted ladybird is known as *Adalia 2-punctata*.

Will blister beetles give you blisters?

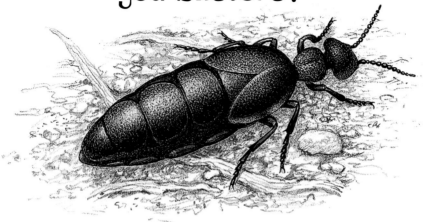

An oil beetle is a type of blister beetle from southern Europe.

Blister beetles live all over the world, but most of them live in warm areas. The adults feed on flowers, and the larvae hitch a ride on passing bees back to their hives to feed on baby bees.

As their name suggests, blister beetles will make your skin very sore if you pick one up. The beetle's blood contains a chemical called cantharidin, which irritates the skin and makes it blister, painfully. The oily blood leaks out of the beetle's knees and other joints when it is handled roughly – or pecked by a bird or gobbled up by a mouse or other predator.

Do you know...?

Cardinal beetles (right) have nasty-tasting blood, too, but it is not as bad as a blister beetle's. The beetle has a bright red body (like the robe of a Catholic cardinal) that warns predators to not try eating the beetle.

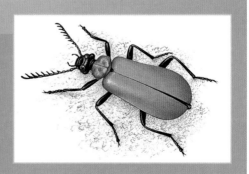

What do darkling beetles do when they get too hot?

A cellar darkling beetle lives in caves, stables and cellars.

Do you know...?

Most darkling beetles are dark coloured. However, on the white sands of some deserts being black would make it too easy for predators to spot them. So these darkling beetles are white. As well as helping them to blend into their surroundings, a white body also helps the beetles to stay cool, by reflecting back much of the hot sunlight.

Darkling beetles live all over the world, but they are most common in deserts, such as the Namib in southern Africa. To survive in the desert, a darkling beetle must be able to withstand very high temperatures. When it gets too hot on the surface, the beetles head underground. They dig by vibrating their legs, which allows them to 'sink' into the sand. They have to dig quickly. The top layer of sand is hot enough to cook them. They have to get to about 3 centimetres down before it is cool enough.

What are a stag beetle's 'antlers'?

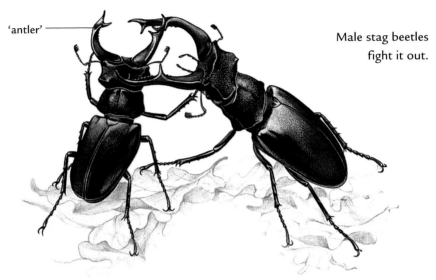

'antler'

Male stag beetles
fight it out.

Only male stag beetles have 'antlers', which are used in fights for access to female mates. Fights are often very short. The male with the shorter antlers will usually give in straight away. The antlers do not grow from the head, but are instead very large mouthparts called mandibles. In most beetles, the mandibles work as pincers to hold and cut up food. However, a stag beetle's giant mandibles can only produce a feeble pinch. So fighting males do not try to cut off their opponents 'antlers'. Instead, they are used to push the other male out of the area.

Do you know...?

Dobsonflies live in the jungles of South America. They have very large mouthparts that are more than half as long as the body in the males (right). However, they are not used for feeding. Instead, the 'horns' are used in tests of strength for mates.

mandible

Why did ancient Egyptians think a scarab beetle pushed the Sun across the sky?

Ancient Egyptians believed in many gods. Each one was responsible for different parts of nature. The Sun god was Ra. He was the most powerful god of all who, the Egyptians believed, had created the world. Ra was helped by Khepri, the god

Scarab beetles roll a ball of dung.

Do you know...?

The largest beetle, and the heaviest insect of all, is the African scarab beetle. The goliath beetle grows to 11 centimetres long and weighs up to 100 grams – that is more than some birds. Despite being so large, goliath beetles can still fly.

of the dawn. It was Khepri's job to push the Sun across the sky each day.

The Egyptians believed that the dawn god took the form of a scarab beetle. These beetles were common in the fields of Egypt, where they rolled the dung of farm animals into balls. The beetles then buried the dung balls and laid their eggs inside them. The beetle grubs hatched out and ate the dung. Although it might sound odd to us, the Egyptians believed that Khepri rolled the Sun through the sky just like a dung beetle rolls dung.

How do Hercules beetles fight?

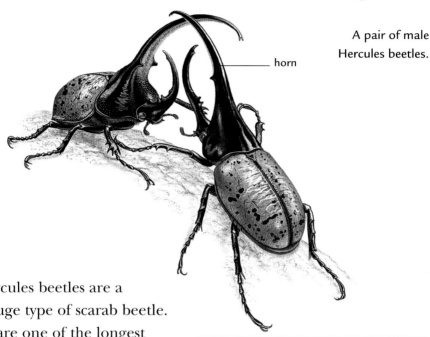

horn

A pair of male Hercules beetles.

Hercules beetles are a huge type of scarab beetle. They are one of the longest beetles in the world. Males grow to a length of 18 centimetres. However, 10 centimetres of that is taken up by an enormous curved horn that sticks out of the back behind the head. A second, shorter horn curves the other way out of the top of the head. These horns are used in fights over the best place to attract females. A male takes up position in a tree and defends it from his rivals. During a fight, the males lock horns and try to knock their opponent over and push him out of the tree.

Do you know...?

The rhinoceros beetle (below) is named after the long horn that grows out of its head. The beetle is the strongest animal for its size on the planet. It can lift 850 times its own weight – that's like a person lifting 65 tonnes!

Why were dung beetles imported to Australia?

When Europeans went to live in Australia, they set up farms to raise cattle and sheep. Soon the country had some of the largest farms in the world. But farming in Australia was not as simple as in other parts of the world. Most of Australia's natural animals are small creatures – there was nothing like a cow living there. So there were also no insects to clean up the cows' dung either. So the cowpats just stayed where they fell, making it hard for grass to grow. The farmers solved the problem by introducing dung beetles from Europe and Africa.

Do you know...?

Australia does have some of its own dung beetles, but they live in a very unusual way. The beetles collect kangaroo poo, but it dries out very quickly. So the beetles climb on to the kangaroo and hang next to its bottom, so they can grab the freshest dung as it appears.

Cattle produce a lot of dung.

Do long-horned beetles actually have horns?

Long-horned beetles use their large antennae to help them balance.

Although several types of beetle do grow horns, long-horned beetles are not among them. In spite of their name, the features growing out of the beetles' heads are antennae, or feelers. The antennae are among the longest in the insect world. The enormous titan beetles of South America have antennae that are 25 centimetres long!

Do you know...?

The harlequin beetle (right) is a type of long-horned beetle that lives in most parts of South America. It gets its name from the vibrant red, yellow and black markings. The colourings look similar to the costume of a harlequin, a medieval clown.

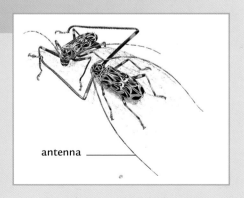

antenna

Why don't potato farmers like Colorado potato beetles?

Colorado potato beetles used to be very rare insects. As their name suggests, they used to live in a small area of Colorado in the south-west of the United States. However, today these little, stripy leaf beetles live across North America, Europe and Asia.

A Colorado potato beetle.

This spread has taken less than 200 years. It began when potatoes were introduced to Colorado. The beetles had always laid their eggs on sandbur, a relative of potato plants, and they laid them on the potatoes, too. The dark-red larvae thrived eating the potato leaves, but they also killed much of the crop. In 1877 the pest made its way to Europe with a shipment of spuds, and soon spread to Asia. However, the beetle is rare in Britain and Ireland.

Do you know...?

Another major insect pest that can devastate entire fields is the boll weevil. This beetle lays its eggs in cotton flowers, which do not produce any fluffy cotton fibre as a result. Boll weevils have caused £8 billion worth of damage in the last 150 years.

Is a weevil's long snout a nose or a mouth?

rostrum

antenna

Weevils are also known as snout beetles.

Weevils are funny-looking beetles. They have long, narrow snouts poking out from their faces. The snout – more correctly called a rostrum – looks like an elephant's trunk. But the rostrum does not have nostrils at the end of it. Instead, its tip is the weevil's tiny mouth.

It is easy to spot a weevil because the insect's antennae, or feelers, always stick out from the side of the rostrum. The adults use their narrow mouths to nibble leaves and wood or to pick up tiny pollen grains. The weevil larvae (young) do not have rostrums. Most of them are chubby grubs that feast on the insides of plants.

Do you know...?

Although they have rostrums like other weevils, toothpick weevils are considered to be a different group of insects. In many species only the female has a long rostrum, which she uses to make holes in bark for her eggs. The males of the species have large mouthparts used during fighting over mates.

rostrum

male

female

CHAPTER 5
MOTHS &
BUTTERFLIES

What is the difference between a moth and a butterfly?

Moths and butterflies form a huge group of insects called the Lepidoptera. That name means 'scale wings', and it refers to the tiny scales that give the wings their patterns.

All moths and butterflies have a normal insect body divided into three sections. They also all have six legs. However, moths tend to come out at night. They usually have drab colouring because their wings are not on show in the dark. Butterflies are daytime flyers. Their wings are often covered in brightly coloured patterns. When a moth lands, it spreads its wings flat. A butterfly holds its wings straight up above its body. Moths often have feathery feelers, or antennae. Butterflies have straight ones with club-shaped tips.

A moth with wings held flat.

A butterfly holds it wings upright.

Do you know...?

Butterflies and moths have a total of four wings. But the front and back wings on each side are hooked together so they work as a single, large wing.

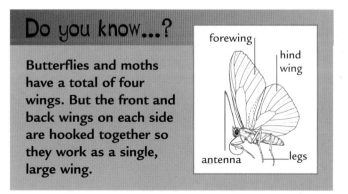
forewing
hind wing
antenna
legs

Which is the largest butterfly in the world?

The largest butterfly in the world is the Queen Alexandra birdwing. This beautiful giant insect lives in New Guinea. The females are larger than the males and can measure up to 28 centimetres across when their wings are held flat.

There are many other species of birdwings living across South-east Asia and

A Queen Alexandra birdwing.

Australia. They are all large compared to other butterflies. Many have beautiful wings, too, and they are highly prized by butterfly collectors. Unfortunately, so many birdwings have been taken from the wild that the largest birdwings, including the Queen Alexandra species, are now in danger of becoming extinct.

Do you know...?

One of the smallest butterflies in the world is the western pygmy blue from North America. Its wingspan – the distance from the tip of one wing to the tip of the other – is just a little more than 1 centimetre.

A common birdwing.

Do swallowtails eat their tails?

A swallowtail butterfly.

With a name like swallowtail, it sounds like these butterflies eat (and swallow) their tails. But that would be a bit silly. Instead, the insects are named after the long tails that stick out of both wings. The forked shape of the two tails makes the butterflies look a little like swallows – fast-flying birds that also have forked tails. Most swallowtails have short tails but these are still easy to see. However, some species have tails that are almost as long as the rest of their bodies.

Do you know...?

Not all swallowtails have tails. The mocker swallowtail has none and it looks very much like a tiger butterfly, which is not a swallowtail. The tiger species has poisons in its body that make anything that eats it feel sick. The mocker hopes to fool predators into leaving it alone.

mocker

tiger butterfly

Where do butterflies find something to drink?

Butterflies 'puddling', or sipping water, on damp ground.

Butterflies and moths drink liquid foods. They drink mainly the nectar from flowers. They may also suck juices from fruits or the sap leaking from trees. Much of this liquid is sweet, but butterflies need salty things, too. They get that by sucking water from damp ground. This behaviour is called 'puddling' and it is most common in dry places. A butterfly may puddle for several hours and drink many times its own body weight as its body removes the salts from the water.

Do you know...?

Butterflies have a long drinking straw for a mouth. The tube is called a proboscis. It is usually kept coiled up under the chin and is unfurled to suck liquid from flowers and fruits.

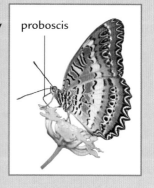

proboscis

How do swallowtail caterpillars scare away ants?

A swallowtail caterpillar has a secret weapon against attack.

Swallowtail caterpillars have a hidden weapon. When they are prodded or poked by a predator, a bright red Y-shaped organ suddenly appears out of its head. This is the osmeterium. Nobody is really sure what it does. It is certainly a surprise when it appears and that might frighten some attackers away. The osmeterium also smells funny. However, birds or wasps do not seem to be put off by it. The most likely function of the osmeterium is to release a smell that is similar to the alarm signal used by ants. That smell makes attacking ants run to their nests.

Do you know...?

The caterpillar of a spicebush swallowtail (below) has an extra way of keeping attackers away – it pretends to be a snake! The caterpillar has dark spots on its head that look like a snake's eyes.

Are white butterflies actually white?

Although the Pieridae family of butterflies is more commonly known as the white, it is, in fact, usually yellow. Many white butterfly species have names that reflect this; these include the sulphurs (a yellow mineral), the brimstones and the orange-tips.

Do you know...?

The cabbage white is a European butterfly. However, today it lives in many other parts of the world – wherever cabbage is grown. The caterpillars (below) eat the cabbage leaves and are serious pests for farmers.

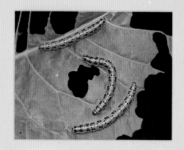

An orange sulphur, a white from North America. This species feeds on alfalfa plants.

Male butterflies are often more brightly coloured than females.

White species range in size from 4 centimetres across to more than 10 centimetres. They have more-rounded wings than most species. You are most likely to see white butterflies in sunny meadows or in a clearing among trees. The males fly around more than the females, often in large groups looking for mates. The females spend more time feeding. They drink the nectar from flowers or suck up salty animal urine.

Why do ants protect blue butterfly caterpillars?

lue butterflies belong to a family called the gossamer-winged butterflies. The group also includes hairstreaks and copper butterflies, which are red-brown in colour. Hairstreaks are named because of the fringe of fine hairs around their wings.

Only male blue butterflies are actually blue. The

A blue butterfly with a fringe of hairs on the wing.

females are brown. Many blues lay their eggs on plants crowded with ants. The ants guard the eggs and caterpillars from attack. In return, the caterpillars release a sweet liquid, which the ants drink.

Do you know...?

A hairstreak butterfly may have a few tails sticking out of its back wings (right). When it lands, the butterfly lifts these tails up so they look like a pair of feelers, or antennae, on a head. That fools predators into attacking the wrong end of the butterfly.

tail

Which is the most common butterfly in the world?

A painted lady.

Many species of butterfly live in just one tiny region of the world. They have evolved to live with all the other plants and animals, that also live there, over millions of years. Many species would struggle to survive anywhere else. However, a few species have managed to set up home all over the world. The most successful of all is the painted lady, which lives on all continents except icy Antarctica. The painted lady is a migrator – it makes long journeys to find better places to feed and breed. That is how it has ended up in so many places. Also, its caterpillars feed on many types of plant, so the insect can usually find something to eat wherever it is.

Do you know...?

The largest species of butterfly is also the rarest. The Queen Alexandra birdwing lives only in the one mountain range in New Guinea.

Why do brush-footed butterflies have just four legs?

A small tortoiseshell butterfly stands on four legs.

All insects have six legs. A creepy-crawly with more or fewer legs than that is not an insect. So how come some butterflies stand on just four legs? The answer is that these insects' front legs have become so short that they are no good for walking. The legs are covered in hairs so they look like little brushes. That is why the largest family of four-legged butterflies are called the brush-foots. The females use their brushes to taste plants and check whether they are suitable for laying their eggs on.

Do you know...?

The red admiral (right) is a common brush-footed butterfly. It is large and easy to spot in gardens and anywhere that has flowers and ripe fruits.

Why are some caterpillars hairy?

A pair of hairy caterpillars.

Have you ever seen a hairy caterpillar? They are often dark-brown or red but they are easy to spot because of the long hairs that stick out from the body. The hairs are not there to keep the caterpillars warm. Instead, they are a caterpillar's defence system, and it is best not to touch them.

Caterpillars have two main threats: wasps that want to lay eggs inside them and predators that want to eat them. Long hairs make it harder for a wasp to get close enough to the caterpillar to lay any eggs. Other hairs have sharp tips that stick into anything that touches the caterpillar. The hair may contain a little bit of poison, or just get stuck under the skin and cause irritation.

Do you know...?

Rajahs are colourful members of the brush-footed butterfly family. Most species have spike-like tails on their wings. The males use these as lances during fights over mates.

How do satyrs shoo away their rivals?

Satyrs are also known as brown butterflies.

Satyrs live in the gloomy world beneath the thick leaf cover of a tropical rainforest. A satyr is always in danger of attack from the predators that lurk in the shadows, but they have a system for reducing the threat. Many satyrs have several 'eyespots' along both wings. These are meant to fool a predator into thinking that they are looking at the face of a much larger animal. However, they also deflect attention from the butterfly's body. Many satyrs have survived attacks; you can see because one or more of the eyespots have been bitten off!

Do you know...?

Satyrs, such as the Scotch argus (right), are very similar to brush-footed butterflies. However, satyrs have thick veins on the forewings that hold sound detectors. These ears are used to pick up the sounds of approaching predators when the butterfly is in the air.

vein

How did the owl butterfly get its name?

Owl butterflies are large insects that live in the forests of Central and South America. Like brush-footed butterflies, they stand on just four legs, and like satyrs they use eyespots to scare off predators. However, owl butterflies rely on a single large spot. The eyespots are ringed with yellow, and in the gloom of the forest that ring makes them flash like the real eye of a dangerous hunter, such as an owl.

Like all butterflies, owl butterflies rest with their wings held upright so only one spot is visible from each side. Some people think the butterfly still looks like a bird's face seen from the side. Others suggest the spot is a decoy that distracts attackers away from the body.

An owl butterfly with a large eyespot on its wing.

Do you know...?

The caterpillars of Caligo owl butterflies are huge. They grow to 11 centimetres long. These caterpillars feed at night but need to stay out of sight during the day. Many hundreds crowd into a funnel-shaped bag made from several leaves glued together with silk. The bags contain caterpillars of all ages, and they work together to maintain their hiding place.

Are a morpho's wings covered in blue scales?

Blue morphos are among the most spectacular insects in the world. They belong to a small group of about 50 big butterflies that live in the forests of South and Central America. Not all morphos are amazing to look at. Many are brown and red. And when it is resting, so does the blue morpho. The undersides of the wings are dull. It is only the males that have shimmering blue on top of the wings. The blue is not created by coloured scales. Instead, it is a pattern formed by the way light reflects off the wing. The surface of the wing has several layers and light reflects in different amounts off all of them. The reflected light then mixes together to form the shimmering colour.

A male blue morpho rests with its wings closed (above) and shows off its blue colours in flight (left).

Do you know...?

Male morphos use their bright wings to attract mates. They patrol an area of forest, giving off flashes of colour as the sun hits their wings. You might think that makes them an easy target for birds, but the morphos 'duck and dive' through the air, making it hard to catch them.

Why have longwings got the largest eyes of any butterfly?

The longwing is the name used for a family of butterflies named the Heliconiidae. Their common name, longwing, comes from the way their wings rise up from their backs, a little like the sails on a yacht.

Longwings live in warm parts of North and South America. In the southern United States and Mexico, many species are known as fritillaries.

A Gulf fritillary feeds on a flower.

Do you know...?

Passion flowers (below) are a favourite food plant for longwings and other butterflies. The caterpillars of most types of longwing butterfly feed on the flowers and leaves, while the adults prefer vines and melon plants.

Many other species come in such a huge range of colours and patterns that it is hard to tell they are related.

Adult longwings drink nectar like most other butterflies. But they can also eat pollen. However, the insects only feed on certain plants. They have large eyes compared to other butterflies so they can see clearly enough to locate their favourite flowers. They prefer the blooms of vines, which have only tiny flowers!

Why do clearwings have see-through wings?

Without scales a butterfly's wing would be see-through, just like those of a fly or a bee. Many different types of butterflies and moths make use of this. They include members of a family of butterflies called the ithomiids that come from South and Central America. These butterflies go by the name of clearwings or transparents – meaning 'see-through'.

You can see straight through this butterfly's scale-less wings.

Having clear wings is a great way to stay out of sight. The insect does not have to pretend to look like the background when the background can be seen right through it.

Do you know...?

A few types of metalmark butterfly have see-through wings. However, most of them have dark bodies (right) with wings covered in shiny metallic scales. Metalmarks are American butterflies. The adults drink nectar or suck up urine, while the caterpillars eat fallen leaves.

Why do monarch butterflies migrate?

A monarch butterfly sets off on its long annual migration.

American monarch butterflies make one of the longest migrations in the insect world. A migration is a journey an animal makes to move to a better place to live or breed. Monarchs spend the summer in the wide open plains of North America. But this region gets cold in winter, so the butterflies head south to sit out the winter in sheltered roosting valleys. There are valleys in California and Florida, but the largest are in Mexico. Each valley contains millions of butterflies. In spring, the surviving insects head north again. Some make a round trip of 4,200 kilometres.

Do you know...?

Male monarchs use hairs on their abdomens (rear sections) to flick a love potion at females. A male must eat special plants before making the potion in glands on his wings. The potion is a sticky liquid that glues to the female's antennae – that is what a butterfly smells with.

A monarch is about 10 centimetres wide.

Why do monarch butterflies eat only milkweeds?

A monarch butterfly feeds on milkweed flowers.

Monarch butterflies belong to a group called the Danaidae family. Most people do not bother with that mouthful and simply call them milkweed butterflies. Most milkweed caterpillars feed on milkweed plants. Some also eat frangipanis where milkweeds do not grow. These plants are poisonous to most animals, but not to the caterpillars. Instead, the caterpillars store the poison in their bodies, which makes them unpleasant to eat. After it eats a caterpillar, a predator will learn not to eat another in a hurry!

Do you know...?

Monarch caterpillars (below) do not need to stay out of sight. They are brightly coloured and it is hard to miss them. The caterpillars are even easier to spot by the way they wave flexible tubes growing out of their heads. The bright colours warn predators that the caterpillars are not good to eat.

Is a skipper a moth or a butterfly?

There is no simple way of telling a moth from a butterfly. So it is not surprising that some members of the Lepidoptera family fall somewhere between the two. The best example of this is the skipper. One feature of moths is that they have bristles between their front and back wings. Butterflies do not have any. Some male skippers have the bristles, while the females of the same species do not. That means the males are moths, while the females are butterflies!

A moth or a butterfly? Let's just call it a skipper.

Do you know...?

Skippers get their name from the way they fly. They make short flights in which they appear to be leaping from plant to plant. To add to the confusion about the skippers' status as moths or butterflies, some fly at night, while others do so in the day.

Skippers are hairier than most butterflies.

Which are the fastest flying insects?

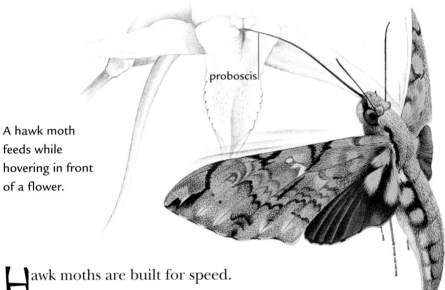

proboscis

A hawk moth feeds while hovering in front of a flower.

Hawk moths are built for speed. Although they are among the heaviest moths of all, these insects are the stunt pilots of the insect world. And they are the fastest flying insects as well.

The moth's heavy weight is down to its huge flying muscles. These allow the moth to beat its wings at an incredible 40 beats per second. The fastest species can hit speeds of 50 kilometres an hour. They could outrun even the world's fastest human sprinters. As well as flying quickly, some hawk moths can do what few other flying animals can do – they can hover in the air!

Do you know...?

Hawk moths have triangular wings (below), which work in the same way as the delta wings of a high-speed jet. The wings allow the moths to make very fast and tight turns in the air.

triangular wing

What is a death's head moth?

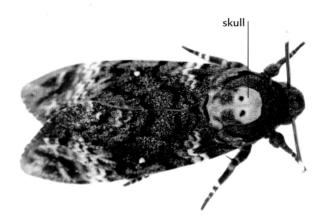

skull

A death's head moth with a skull shape on its back.

Do you know...?

Adult death's head moths have a sweet tooth. At night they drink sugary nectar from flowers, like thousands of other species. However, that is not enough for the death's heads. They also creep into bees' nests (below) and steal the honey.

The name death's head moth is used for three species of hawk moth. All three live in the Mediterranean region, with some also living in western Asia, northern Europe or parts of Africa. The moths earn their name from the markings on the dark back of the adult moth that look a bit like a human skull!

The three species have different scientific names, but they all have a spooky theme: one is named after the Greek goddess in charge of making sure people died at the right time; another is named after the river between the real world and the land of the dead; the third is named after a goddess in charge of how long someone lived for.

What will happen to a wasp-infected caterpillar?

A hawk moth caterpillar carries a load of wasp eggs. Is that a good thing?

It is not easy being a caterpillar. Although they have little else to do other than eat as much as possible, most caterpillars do not stay alive long enough to make the change into an adult moth or butterfly. The caterpillars are not just in danger from birds or other predators snatching them from leaves; tiny wasps are also a big problem. These wasps do not sting caterpillars. They do something even worse – they lay eggs on or inside their bodies. And when the eggs hatch, the caterpillars will be eaten alive from the inside out!

Do you know...?

Several types of caterpillar look like a snake, but the larvae (young) of hawk moths go one step further. When under threat, they curl their head and middle body sections into an S-shape and sway from side to side. Although they are a lot shorter than a real snake, this snake impression is enough to scare off most attackers.

Why do sphinx moths like white flowers?

Sphinx moth is the name used for some hawk moths. Most, although not all, sphinx moths fly at night. They drink nectar from flowers. Some have a very long proboscis (feeding tube), which can reach right into funnel-shaped flowers. Others have shorter tubes and only land

A sphinx moth feeds on nectar at night.

on flowers with nectarines (nectar stores) that are easy to get to.

Many flowers are built to attract insects. These animal visitors transfer pollen between blooms as part of the plants' breeding system. Many flowers attract visitors with bright colours, but colours are not visible at night. So the flowers that attract night-feeding animals, such as moths and bats, are normally white. Instead, the moths are guided to the blooms in the darkness by their powerful scents.

Do you know...?

Many sphinx moths do not land on flowers. They can hover instead. However, other insects cannot do this. So most flowers are built as wide landing platforms (below) for their insect visitors.

Which is the largest moth?

The atlas moths of Asia and Australia are the largest moths in the world. They are a staggering 30 centimetres across. That also makes them the largest of any type of lepidopteran with a wingspan that is greater than even the birdwing butterflies. Like the birdwings, the atlas moths are rare because so many have been taken from the wild by collectors.

Atlas moths are the giants of the moth world.

Atlas moths are the largest members of a small family called the giant silkworm moths. As their name suggests, these moths are all on the large side, and many also have spectacular colourings. As well as the atlas moths, this family also includes species with grand names like emperor moths and royal moths.

How can you spot a male luna moth?

Luna moths live in North America, where they are among the largest moths. They are quite easy to see because they are attracted to the outside lights on people's houses. They often perch on walls of homes.

The luna moths are relatives of atlas moths and other giants from elsewhere in the world.

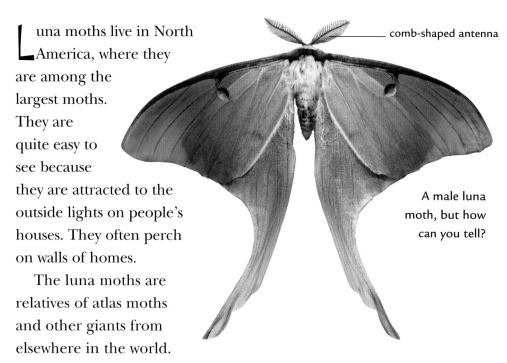

comb-shaped antenna

A male luna moth, but how can you tell?

They are only 10 centimetres across, but the moths make up for their small size by some beautiful colourings and impressive curved tails.

Do you know...?

Luna moths belong to the giant silkworm moth family. Like true silkworms, the moth's caterpillars make fine silk fibres. Some American species (right) are used as a cheap source of silk fibres.

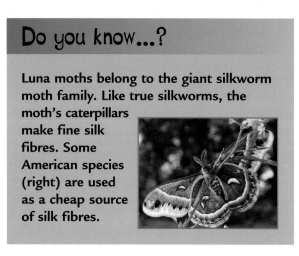

Both male and female luna moths have the same green, brown and purple wings. However, male luna moths have comb-shaped antennae (feelers), which are used to pick up the scent of females. The females have straight antennae.

Why have peppered moths changed colour?

Most peppered moths have a black and white pattern that lets them hide on tree trunks covered in lichens with the same colours. However, a few moths are completely black. During England's Industrial Revolution in the 1800s, forests became polluted with smoke from the many new factories. That killed the lichens on the trees, making it hard for the black and white moths to hide. But the black varieties had no problem and they became common near factories. This is used by biologists as an example of how evolution can change a species.

The peppered moth on the left is most common in unpolluted areas, while the dark one on the right is found in polluted forests.

Do you know...?

Peppered moths belong to a group called the measuringworm moths. They get this name from inchworms, the common name for their caterpillars (below). The caterpillars move with large, curling steps, as if they were measuring out an inch every time.

How do we make silk from worms?

Silk clothing is very luxurious and expensive. It was first made in China 4500 years ago, and its production has been a closely guarded secret for much of that time. Today we know that silk is made by silkworms. In fact, these are not actually worms but moth caterpillars.

Do you know...?

The silkworm moth (below) no longer lives in the wild. It only survives in the silk factories, where its caterpillars are raised on mulberry leaves before their cocoons are turned into luxury material.

Silkworm cocoons are made from silk fibres.

The finest silks are made by the caterpillars of a moth called *Bombyx mori*. These caterpillars are bred in huge numbers in silk factories. They are allowed to spin silk cocoons but that is as far as they get. The cocoons are boiled in water or baked to kill the insects inside. Then the cocoons' silk is unravelled. It does not go very far. It takes 3,000 silkworms to make just 1 kilogram of finished silk.

How do tent caterpillars build a tent?

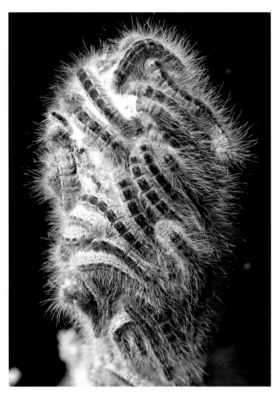

A crowd of tent caterpillars gather together for safety during the day.

Tent caterpillars are the young of a group of moths that live in warm parts of the world. The caterpillars live in large crowds. That keeps them safe from attack. By night, the caterpillars raid trees. Together they can strip the bark off an entire trunk. At dawn, the moths head home to a tent-like nest made from silk. All the residents have contributed to this tent. The caterpillars in a tent are related and they help each other to find food. Foraging caterpillars leave scent trails to lead the others to food.

Do you know...?

Processionary moth caterpillars also gather together for safety. They hang silk nests in pine and oak trees. At dusk, when it is time to feed, the moths file out of the nest one by one, forming a procession – hence their name.

An adult tent caterpillar moth.

How do tiger moths use foam to scare off attackers?

A great tiger moth.

Tiger moths are very brightly coloured for a moth. They live in the warm parts of the world. Many of the adult moths do not feed. They concentrate on finding a mate and laying eggs. The caterpillars feed on lichens and many different plants. Much of this food contains poisons. The caterpillars store the poisons and they are still there when the insects change into adults.

When an adult tiger moth is attacked, it releases these poisons in the form of a foamy liquid that spills out of a gland in the centre of the body. The foam smells and tastes bad, and predators suddenly lose their appetite for tiger moths!

Do you know...?

It is not just moths that are named after tigers. There are tiger butterflies, too (below). Tiger butterflies live in the Americas. Many of their caterpillars are pests on potato farms.

How does a tiger moth confuse a bat?

This bat is sleeping, but soon it will be out looking for prey – including moths.

Bats find prey by making high-pitched squeaks that bounce off flying insects. The bats can tell where their prey is by listening to the echoes. Tiger moths have got wise to this. They listen out for the bats' calls and then make their own squeaks. The bats hear a moth's squeaks and know that the moth they are tracking is filled with poisons. The bats veer away from their attack and search for a more tasty meal in the darkness.

Do you know...?

Caterpillars are usually causing problems for farmers, not solving them. But that is exactly what the caterpillars of cinnabar moths (right) did in New Zealand. Ragweed was poisoning cattle in that country, so the caterpillars were introduced to keep this dangerous plant in check.

Why do owlet moths lay their eggs in spiders' webs?

The common name
of this owlet moth is
sweetheart underwing.

The owlet moths
form the largest family
of moths, with 25,000 species
living in all parts of the world.
Most species of owlet moth lay
their eggs directly on a plant that
the caterpillars can eat as soon as
they hatch. However, a few species
opt to leave the eggs in the care
of a spider, who has built a web
in a suitable plant. The moths
climb on to the web to lay eggs.
The spider does not seem to
be bothered by the invaders.

When the eggs hatch, the
caterpillars spend most of their
time lying motionless in their
silken home so they do not disturb
their spider host. The caterpillars
only crawl off the web when they
need to eat the fresh leaves nearby.

Do you know...?

Many of the caterpillars of
owlet moths are farm pests.
The most damaging insects
have names
such as
cutworms
(right) or
armyworms.
Cutworms
attack wheat,
cabbage,
corn and
carrots. The
armyworm is
a pest of
tomatoes and
potatoes.

Why shouldn't you touch a tussock moth caterpillar?

A fully grown tussock moth before it forms a cocoon.

Tussock moth caterpillars have four brushes of hair on their backs. There are also long, black hairs on their heads. The hairs are a defence system. Touching the hairs causes an itchy rash on the skin. The caterpillars also have a gland that releases chemicals as a second line of defence. The hairs are left in the cocoon after the caterpillar has changed into an adult. Eggs are laid among the hairs for protection.

Do you know...?

The female rusty tussock moth does not have wings. She attracts a mate with scent after emerging from her cocoon. Then she lays her eggs inside the empty cocoon. The eggs stay warm inside the cocoon all through winter before hatching in spring.

Black arches tussock moths.

What happened when gypsy moths were introduced to the United States?

A female gypsy moth lays eggs under a layer of protective brown felt.

Gypsy moths are one of the most destructive insect pests in history. They are a European species, but the moths were brought to North America by mistake in 1869. The moths spread quickly across a huge area of forest. They had no problem adapting to the different trees in America. Soon their caterpillars were stripping the bark from entire forests. They have few predators in America, and they can cause many millions of pounds worth of damage each year. And the moths are still spreading!

Do you know...?

When a forest is under attack by gypsy moth caterpillars, it is possible to hear the chewing sounds created by hundreds of thousands of tiny jaws at work.

A gypsy moth caterpillar.

How is a burnet moth caterpillar like a slug?

A slug caterpillar.

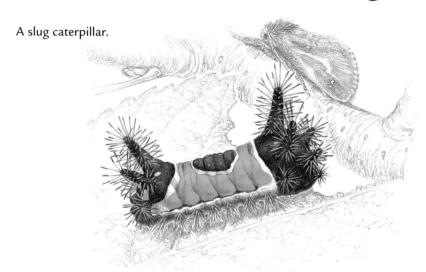

As their name suggests, the caterpillars of slug-caterpillar moths are unusual young. Most caterpillars walk on legs and other leg-like appendages (outgrowths). However, the slug caterpillars move more like a slug or a snail, which has no legs just a single 'foot'. Unlike other caterpillars, the underside of a slug caterpillar does not have any legs. Instead, it has fleshy suckers that stick the caterpillar to a leaf. The suckers are moved forwards in turn to drag the caterpillar forwards. From above, it looks like the animal is sliding along in the same way as a slug.

Do you know...?

It may not look like it, but caterpillars have only six legs, like adult insects. They also walk on fleshy stumps called prolegs, but these are lost when the caterpillar changes into an adult.

leg

proleg

What is a bagworm?

A bagworm drags its house up a grass stem.

Bagworm moths live on the move and build mobile homes out of whatever they can find around them. The caterpillars, or bagworms, build the house. They glue together grasses, leaves and flakes of wood or bark with silk. Some species build cases out of sand grains, while others construct neat houses of sticks. The caterpillar drags its home along as it feeds. There is even a back door for its droppings to fall out through. The bagworm uses its case as a cocoon. Adult males fly off in search of mates, but the female moths have no wings, so cannot fly. They live in the case and lay their eggs in it before dying.

Do you know...?

Clothes moths are a very common household pest. Their caterpillars feed on wool, skin, dust and other natural materials used in the home. Like bagworms, the caterpillars make protective cases out of the fibres. Some of the cases can be quite colourful thanks to the modern dyes used on fabrics.

CHAPTER 6
BEES & WASPS

Why do some bumblebees bury themselves before they die?

A bumblebee collects food from a flower.

When a bumblebee lands on a flower to collect some nectar or pollen, there might be another insect waiting for the bee. A female wasp fly uses the body of a bumblebee as a nursery for its young. The wasp fly swoops on the bee in mid-air and lays an egg inside the bee. The egg hatches into a maggot that eats the bee's insides. The maggot is careful what it eats, and the bee does not die straightaway. Before the maggot kills the bee, it makes it bury itself in the ground. There the maggot will be safe through the winter before changing into an adult in spring.

Do you know...?

The stripes of a wasp fly (below) make it look a little like a bee or a wasp. The adult flies feed on flowers, which are good places for them to find a carrier for their eggs.

Will a giant horntail give you a nasty sting?

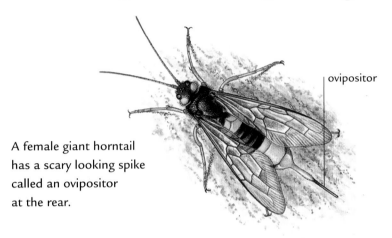

ovipositor

A female giant horntail has a scary looking spike called an ovipositor at the rear.

The giant horntail is a large type of sawfly. Sawflies are relatives of bees, wasps and ants. The horntail and many other sawflies have the familiar yellow and black colouring of stinging wasps and bees. Many other species are less brightly coloured. However, sawflies can look frightening because the females have spike-like 'tails' sticking out of their abdomens (rear sections). However, this spike is not a stinger. Unlike some wasps, bees and ants, sawflies cannot sting. Instead, the spike, known as an ovipositor, is a tube for laying eggs. A sawfly's ovipositor has a sharp, saw-shaped edge, which the sawfly uses to cut into wood. The eggs are laid in the wood.

Do you know...?

Unlike its cousins – the bees, ants and wasps – a sawfly larva (young, below) is not raised in a nest. Instead, it looks and lives more like a caterpillar.

Why do some wasps lay eggs inside other insects?

Everyone has been close to a yellow and black wasp – often too close! However, these stinging insects are not typical of wasps. Most wasps do not sting. Instead of a stinger, they have a long tube, or ovipositor, for laying eggs. Some wasps use their sharp ovipositors to lay their eggs inside wood or far down into the ground. However, most of them stick their sharp tubes into the body of another animal, usually another insect.

The eggs hatch into larvae (young), which eat whatever there is around them, including living bodies. The larvae eventually kill their victims. An animal that survives in this way is called a parasitoid.

An ichneumon wasp lays eggs in wood.

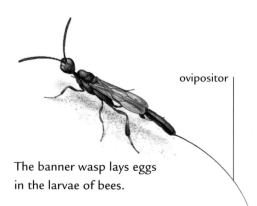

ovipositor

The banner wasp lays eggs in the larvae of bees.

Do you know...?

A parasite lives on or in another animal. Many wasps are a type of parasite called a parasitoid because they eventually kill their victims. Some wasps are hyperparasites – parasites of parasites. They lay their eggs inside larvae that are themselves already inside another animal!

How do gall wasps make plants swell up?

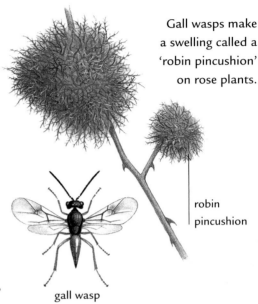

Gall wasps make a swelling called a 'robin pincushion' on rose plants.

robin pincushion

gall wasp

A swelling on a plant is called a gall. They come in many shapes and sizes. Some look like hairy growths, others like large lumps, while some look like tiny apples. Galls are made by a plant's defence system. They grow after tiny gall wasps lay their eggs inside the plant. When the eggs hatch, the plant reacts to them by growing a gall, which gives the young insects somewhere to live and a supply of food. But it also stops the insects from spreading to other parts of the plant. Each species of gall wasp attacks just one species of plant.

Do you know...?

Figs could not grow without fig wasps. Fig wasps lay eggs inside the fig. The larvae feed inside. When they become adults, they leave the fig, taking some pollen with them. The wasps then cut into a new fig to lay eggs and leave the pollen. At the same time, some pollen is left inside, so the plant can reproduce. The pollen develops into the fig's seeds.

How did the cuckoo wasp get its name?

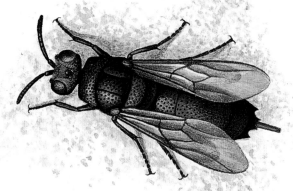

An adult cuckoo wasp.

A cuckoo is a bird that lays an egg in the nest of another bird. The cuckoo flies away and leaves its chick to be raised by a completely unrelated bird from another species. This behaviour is used by other animals too, including the cuckoo wasps. These small shiny insects lay their eggs inside the nests of other wasps and bees. The larvae eat the eggs and young already living there. The female cuckoo wasps have to be tough to get into a bee's nest because the nests are heavily guarded. If attacked, the cuckoo wasp rolls into a ball so only its heavily armoured back is showing.

Do you know...?

Digger wasps are large bees. The yellow-faced digger wasp (below) is 4 centimetres long; it is the largest type of bee or wasp in Europe. Digger wasps get their name from the way the female burrows into the ground to find a beetle grub to lay her eggs inside.

Why do spider wasps bury paralysed spiders?

A European spider-hunting wasp preys on wolf spiders.

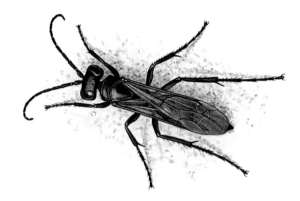

Spiders are fierce hunters, but they are no match for the weaponry of a spider wasp. Even large, hairy tarantulas cannot escape a spider wasp. Adult spider wasps feed on flower nectar but use the body of a spider as a food supply for their young. The wasp normally attacks a spider on the ground. It stings the spider, pumping a powerful venom (poison) into it. That paralyses the spider – but does not kill it. The wasp then crams the helpless spider into a burrow and lays a few eggs on top. Soon the larvae (young wasps) will be eating the spider alive.

A spider wasp takes on a tarantula.

Do you know...?

You would think that a spider that lives in water would be safe from a spider wasp. Wrong! When a fisher spider dives to escape the wasp, the insect swims down after it and stings it under water. The wasp then lifts its victim to the surface and hauls it to the bank. The spider is then buried in the wasp's nest inside a mouse's burrow.

Why do wasps have black and yellow stripes?

The most common European wasp is called the German yellow jacket.

The yellow and black striped wasps that seem to be everywhere on hot days are known as social wasps. They live in large, crowded nests and work together to raise young. It might come as a surprise to learn that only 4,000 species of the 120,000 types of wasp live in this way. However, social wasps, or yellow jackets as they are sometimes known, are the only wasps that regularly sting people. Their yellow and black markings are easy to see, and we learn to leave these striped insects alone from a young age.

Do you know...?

The social wasps that fly into houses or turn up uninvited at picnics are all females. A nest of wasps is filled with many thousands of sisters. They all work together to raise yet more sisters from eggs produced by the wasps' single mother: the queen.

Wasp stings are painful but they are very rarely dangerous.

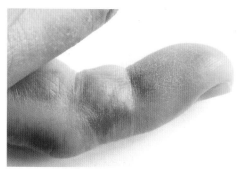

Do paper wasps make nests from paper?

Paper is made by crushing up soft wood and mixing it with water to make a mush, or pulp. This pulp can be rolled into sheets and, once dried, becomes a piece of paper.

Most social wasps build their nests from paper, and they make it themselves in the same sort of way as we do. The wasp scrapes bits off a dead branch using its mouth. Soon it has a ball of fibres, which is mixed with saliva (spit). That makes the wood fibres into pulp, which the wasp can use to make almost any shape it wants. When the pulp dries it feels a lot like paper. The nest is light enough to hang from a single stalk glued to a branch or overhang. However, the internal structure of the nest makes it surprisingly tough.

A wasp nest is made up of six-sided rooms, or cells.

Do you know...?

Some wasps from South America make nests from a see-through material that looks like cellophane. The nesting material is made from a liquid that the wasps release from their bodies.

How does a wasp colony begin?

Wasp colonies begin as a small nest at first.

It takes just one wasp to start a colony – the queen. The queen will have mated with several males after leaving her mother's nest a few days before. Before she has some daughters to work for her, the young queen must build the first part of the nest herself. In some species she may be joined by other new queens – most of these late arrivals will be her sisters.

The team are soon ready to raise their first brood of young. All of this first brood will have been produced by just one of the queens. She became dominant by biting and stinging the others and releasing chemicals that stopped them from laying their own eggs.

The queen behaves in the same way to her daughters. Soon they are caring for the nest, while the queen concentrates on laying eggs.

Do you know...?

A cuckoo queen is a wasp that belongs to a different species which pushes its way into a wasp nest and does away with the original queen. The worker wasps do not even notice what is going on and continue working for the new queen.

What do wasps eat?

A wasp takes a drink of apple juice.

The answer to this question is simple: nothing at all – they can only drink. Adult wasps can only swallow liquids, so they feed mainly on nectar from flowers and juices that ooze from fruits or plant stems.

Wasp larvae (young) can swallow solid food, but they rely entirely on what forager wasps bring back to the nests. Foragers collect bits of leaf and pollen or they may kill smaller insects with their jaws. The food is passed to a nursing wasp, which sucks out any liquid for herself before holding it out for the larvae to munch on.

Do you know...?

Wasp larvae do not leave their cells until they become adults (below). If they want food they beg for it by scraping their mouths on the paper walls of the cells. A worker bee soon answers the call with a piece of food.

Do all stinging wasps live in colonies?

A fly-hunting wasp kills a fly for its larva which it eats.

Some wasps like to live alone. However, many of these so-called solitary wasps are seldom far from each other. Instead, they each make a nest in an area to create an immense city of wasps. In a few cases, several females work together to build an 'apartment building' with several nests in it. This is similar to what social wasps do. But the big difference is that all the solitary females lay eggs in their own nests. The solitary wasps can sting, but they use their mouths to kill prey. This prey is packed away inside the nest for the wasp larvae (young) to feed on.

Do you know...?

One of the largest hunting wasps in the world is the cicada-killing wasp. This insect from North America is 4 centimetres long. It lives alone in nests under the ground. But thousands of wasps may nest next to each other, causing damage to lawns. The wasps stock up larders for their larvae with cicadas (below).

What do wool-carder bees make their nests from?

A male wool-carder bee.

Wool-carder bees do not live in hives or large nests containing thousands of bees. Instead, each female bee makes her own nest in a small crack in a wall or in a notch in a tree trunk. She lines the ragged and sharp walls of the nest with fluff that she has 'carded', or combed, from the surrounding area. She scrapes the surface of hairy leaves and stems to strip them of their furry covering. The fluff is also used to plug the cells of developing larvae (young).

Do you know...?

A mason is a person who works with stone. A mason bee does not do that exactly but makes nests from mud instead. The bees collect the mud from the edges of ponds and mix it with saliva.

The carder bumblebee also lines its nest with leaf fibres.

What do mining bees fill their burrows with?

Have you ever seen tiny piles of soil on a lawn? They are most common in spring. Each one is the excavation of a mining bee. The entrance to its burrow will be near to the mound. If it is fine weather, the bee might even be sunning itself at the entrance.

Only a female mining bee digs a burrow, which is a home for her larvae (young). The nest branches into several chambers. The adult bee stocks each room with a mixture of pollen and honey. She then hangs a single egg on the chamber wall above the mixture. When the larva hatches, it will fall into the food mixture and will never go hungry.

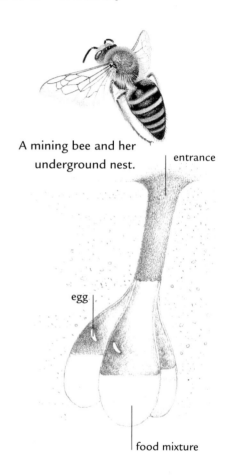

A mining bee and her underground nest.

entrance

egg

food mixture

Do you know...?

Carpenter bees are large, round bees with hairy bodies. They are sometimes mistaken for bumblebees. However, a carpenter bee (right) makes her nest by digging into the wood of a dead tree – or the frame of a house. The bee lays huge eggs – about half the size of mum!

A male honeybee, or drone.

What happens to a male honeybee during mating?

Male honeybees are rare. All the worker bees in a hive are females. The workers are the daughters of the queen bee, and they look after their young sisters for their mother. Male honeybees, or drones, are only born when it is time to mate and start a new nest. The queen lays a special brood of eggs that become drones and one new queen. These offspring fly off and mate with other bees from nearby hives. The queen mates with several drones before heading back to take over her mother's nest. The drones mate only once. They release sperm with such force that they explode!

Do you know...?

A drone is raised in a cell in the hive's honeycomb just like his sisters, the workers. However, his cell is wider than the others. The queen bee feels the size of the cell and lays an unfertilised egg in it. This type of egg, which will always grow into a male, contains only half the number of genes as the eggs that grow into females. That number of genes is all a male needs to mate with a future queen.

Can killer bees really kill?

Killer bee is the name used to describe a breed of honeybee that lives in warm parts of North and South America. The better name for them is Africanised bee. These bees exist because of an accident. In 1956 a Brazilian scientist decided to breed honeybees with another species from Africa. He hoped the new species would make more honey in hot places – like Brazil.

Killer bees have spread across a huge area in just 50 years.

But, his experiments failed and the 'Africanised' bees escaped into the wild. The bees do not have more powerful stings than normal honeybees, it is just that they are more likely to use them. Africanised bees are not fussy about where they live, and so their swarms often end up in places that are near to people. If disturbed, Africanised bees sting in huge numbers. If a person cannot run away they may be killed by the poison in the thousands of stings.

Do you know...?

Honeybees form a swarm (right) when the hive becomes too crowded. Half of the bees leave the hive along with the old queen to find a new place to live. A young queen takes over the old nest.

How do honeybees make honey?

Honeybees live for six weeks and they are busy for every minute.

oneybees do not make honey for us. Honey is food for their larvae (young), which are born at a rate of 2,000 a day. The honey also keeps the colony going through the winter.

Honey is made from nectar. A forager bee delivers a droplet of nectar to another worker, who 'ripens' it by letting some of the water evaporate. The nectar is then stored in a cell in the hive. Other bees drive away more water by fanning the cell with their wings until the cell is filled with thick and sticky honey.

Do you know...?

There can be 80,000 worker bees in a single hive. A worker's job depends on how old it is. Young workers are house bees. They produce wax for building and royal jelly for the larvae. It is also the house bees' job to make honey.

133

Why do bee-keepers use smoke?

Bee-keepers work in protective clothing.

Bee-keeping can be a painful job. Even the most expert bee-keeper gets a painful sting from time to time. No one blames the bees for trying to stop a bee-keeper from harvesting their hard-earned honey.

However, a bee-keeper has a clever trick to make his job easier. He blows thick smoke into the nest. The bees do not realise they are living in a wooden box made for them by the bee-keeper. They think they are in a normal nest in a woodland, and the smoke is coming from trees that are on fire. The bees dash into the middle of the hive and begin to eat the honey before the nest is destroyed by fire. They are so busy they do not realise that the bee-keeper is removing the honey until it is too late.

Do you know...?

It is not just people who like honey. The honey badger is also a big fan. It is led to bees' nests by a bird called the honeyguide. The tough badger smashes into the nest to get at the sweet honey, while its bird partner pecks at the wax used to make the nest's honeycomb.

Why does a bee dance?

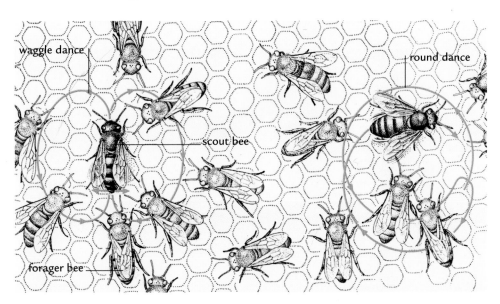

waggle dance

round dance

scout bee

forager bee

Older worker bees have the most risky job – collecting food from flowers. These foragers do not just set off each morning and see what they turn up. They wait for scout bees to fly home from a tour of the area. The scouts give directions to good sources of food using 'dances'. If the food is less than 25 metres away, the scouts do the 'round dance'. They make more turns if the food is especially rich in sugar. The scouts use the 'waggle dance' to show the whereabouts of food that is 100 metres away. This dance gives both distance and direction. A combination of the two dances directs foragers to food that is between the two distances.

Scout bees dance to show the foragers where the food is.

Do you know...?

Honeybees collect pollen to carry back to the nest. They pack it in pollen baskets on their hind legs (below).

How does a young honeybee become a queen?

Workers tend to bee larvae growing in the cells in the hive. Will one become queen?

The honeybees that look after the larvae (young), produce a thick liquid from a gland on their heads called royal jelly. Biologists also refer to it as 'bee milk' because it is not just the 'royal' queens that eat it. Every developing larva gets a little bit of the jelly mixed in with their diet of pollen. However, the larva that is to become the nest's next queen is fed nothing but bee milk. Bee milk is a highly nutritious food, and the royal larva grows to twice the size of a worker bee. If two or more new queens are reared at the same time, they will fight to the death until a single winner remains.

Do you know...?

The queen does not feed young or maintain the nest but she is very busy. She patrols the nest, laying eggs in empty cells. Her patrol also spreads her scent through the nest. This smell lets the workers know who's boss.

CHAPTER 7
ANTS

How do weaver ants weave their nests?

Weaver ants are normally red-brown, but Australian ones are green.

Weaver ants live in forest trees, where they make nests out of leaves. They construct their nests by folding leaves to make parcel shapes. A small nest might be made of a single folded leaf, while big ones are made from 20 leaves and measure 30 centimetres across. The ants work in teams to build these structures. The worker ants form insect chains as they pull the leaf edges together. Other workers use tacky silk to gum the leaves together. This silk is made by the ants' larvae (young), which are carried through the construction site like glue sticks.

Do you know...?

Honeypot ants are an Australian species that have an unusual way of storing food. Some workers are stuffed with food, which is converted into a sweet liquid, a bit like honey. The ants' rear ends swell up, forming huge sacs of liquid. Other ants feed on the liquid dripping from the sacs.

Can velvet ants kill a cow?

A velvet ant is named after the shiny hairs on its body.

Velvet ants are large orange and black insects. Despite the name, velvet ants are actually a type of wasp. They spend the first part of their lives as uninvited guests in bees' nests, where they eat baby bees. Adult female velvet ants do not have wings, which is why they were first thought to be large ants. The females also have powerful stings. Each female's sting is almost half as long as her body. It is jabbed into skin if the velvet ant is handled badly. The sting makes a painful swelling. An American species is nicknamed the 'cow killer' because of its powerful sting, although it is not a danger to cows themselves. People have died from such stings, but these cases were probably allergic reactions.

Is this cow safe from a velvet ant? Probably.

Do you know...?

Male velvet ants have wings. They are often much bigger than the females as well. Some males whisk females off their feet and carry them into the air so that they can mate.

Leaf-cutter ants head back to the nest.

What do leaf-cutter ants do with the leaves?

Leaf-cutter ants are fun insects to watch. Most of them live in tropical rainforests, but you might see them at the zoo or on the television. The ants head out from their underground nests, along crowded highways that cut across the forest floor, and up into the trees. There, the ants cut sections of green leaves with their mouths. A section is often several times the size of the ant. The ants carry the leaves back to the nest, where they are piled into compost heaps. The ants clean the leaves before chewing them into pulp. The pulp is then 'planted' with fungus. The ants tend the underground gardens and harvest the fungus for food.

Do you know...?

The ants in a colony work together to find food, raise the young and protect the queen. But some ants have come up with a way to escape all the hard work. These ants raid the nests of other species, steal their young and make them slaves. The slaves do everything – they even die defending the nest from attack.

Do ants ever have wings?

A carpenter ant prepares to fly off and look for a mate.

If you've ever looked inside an ant's nest you will see that none of the insects have wings. However, about once a year swarms of winged ants emerge from most nests. The larger ones are young queens that will start new colonies elsewhere. The smaller ants are males, which fly off to find a queen to mate with. The queen mates just once – but that is enough to make all of the millions of daughter ants she will produce in her life. The male dies after mating, while the queen loses her wings before setting up home.

A pair of ants mating.

Do you know...?

All male ants do is mate. They do not help in the nest. They are born with only half the genes of female ants. But that is all a queen ant needs from her mate.

What is the largest ant nest?

Ants are everywhere – they are the most common type of insect. If you made all the world's animals into a huge lump, about a fifth of it would be made of only ants. That is more than all the mammals, such as whales, cattle and people, put together!

Most ants live in colonies containing many thousands or millions of individuals. Some ant species live in supercolonies, where

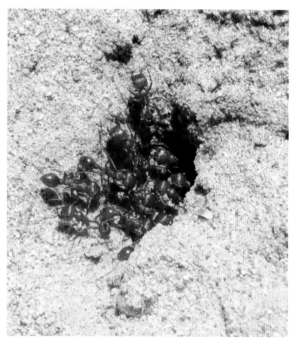

Ant colonies are made up of thousands of sisters, who are worker ants for their mother, the queen.

several nests are merged together. A worker from one nest is allowed to live in any of the others in the supercolony. The largest supercolony ever discovered is in Southern Europe. It is 6,000 kilometres wide and has more than a million nests in it. Its number of ants runs into the billions.

Which are the largest ants in the world?

Not all the ants in a colony do the same job or look the same. For example, tiny leaf-cutter ants, called minims, clean the leaves brought back by the larger workers. The largest ant in the nest is the queen. And she is the most deadly, with the power to kill any member of her colony. But the queen leaves most of the fighting to her soldier ants. These are larger than the workers and they are armed with powerful jaws.

The largest ants in the world are bullet ants from South America. The workers are 2 centimetres long, and the queen is twice this size. There are no soldiers in the colony. Instead, each worker has a sting strong enough to kill a person.

A soldier ant.

Do you know...?

Fire ants (below) are a major pest in North America. Not only do they damage crops, but they can also give a nasty sting. Their name comes from the way the sting burns the skin.

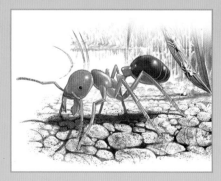

How do worker ants know what to do next?

Worker ants always seem to know what they should be doing. Working!

Acolony of ants is a very effective team. The ants communicate using scents, called pheromones. A scout ant that has found a supply of food near the nest will lay a trail of pheromones for workers to follow. A pheromone is also used to warn the colony of danger. When one ant is attacked, it produces an alarm scent. Other ants nearby smell the signal and release the same scent as they run to help. Soon hundreds of ants are rushing to defend the nest.

Ants stroke each other's faces when they meet.

Do you know...?

Some worker ants lay eggs that never hatch. However, if the queen dies, one of the egg-producing workers will be promoted to queen. Then her eggs will hatch.

CHAPTER 8
OTHER INSECTS
& RELATIVES

How does a springtail jump?

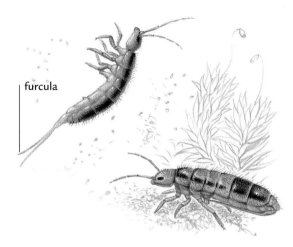

furcula

Springtails live hidden away in damp places.

Springtails are tiny creepy-crawlies, but they are not a type of insect. They do share many features with insects, such as having six legs. However, insects have three distinct body sections: the head, the thorax (mid-body) and the abdomen (rear end). Many insects also have wings. But a springtail's body does not have these sections and it never has wings.

Instead of flying, springtails jump. The other big difference between springtails and insects is the springtail's furcula. This is a forked tail that folds under the body. The furcula is the springtail's jumping organ. It jumps by flicking the furcula underneath the body so it pushes down on the ground and launches the springtail into the air.

Do you know...?

You might have never seen one, but you will have been surrounded by springtails at many times in the past. In damp places, such as woodlands (below), there are at least 7,500 springtails in every square metre!

Can a silverfish swim?

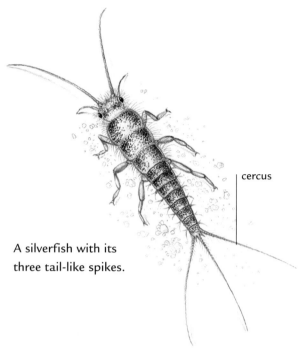

cercus

A silverfish with its three tail-like spikes.

Silverfish are not fish. They do not even live in water and they cannot swim. Instead, these creatures are a primitive type of insect. Biologists think that the first insects looked and lived a bit like silverfish.

Silverfish get their name from the colour of the scales that cover their backs. They live in warm and damp places. Silverfish often take up home close to heating pipes in large buildings, where they eat almost anything they can find. For this reason, silverfish are also known as fire brats.

Silverfish do not have wings. Their most obvious features are the three tail-like spikes that stick out of their rear ends. The middle one is a part of the insect's abdomen (rear body section). The two outer spikes are growths called cerci (plural of cercus).

How long does an adult mayfly live for?

Adult mayflies are very delicate animals. They have four wings and three long 'tails' sticking out of their rear ends. However, young mayflies – known as nymphs – do not look like this. They live underwater so they do not need wings. The three 'tails' are shorter and feathery to help the insects paddle through the water.

Mayflies spend most of their lives as nymphs. They spend a year in the water before climbing into the air. They then shed their skin, or moult, in two stages to become adults. All an adult male mayfly needs to do is find a mate. That does not take very long and just two hours later the male insect dies. The females survive a little longer, perhaps as much as a few days. In that time, each female must lay her eggs in the water.

Although it is not a larva any more, this insect is not yet a fully mature adult mayfly.

Do you know...?

Adult mayflies do not have time to eat. And that is just as well because they do not have mouths! The insects do all their eating as nymphs, which scrape mouthfuls from water plants with their sharp mouthparts.

How do dragonflies see?

A dragonfly's eyes cover most of its head.

Dragonflies are fierce hunters that catch other insects in mid-air. To do this they need to be expert flyers and to have excellent eyesight. A dragonfly's eyes allow it to see all around. An insect's eyes work in a different way to our own. They are compound eyes. Each eye is actually 28,000 smaller units. Each unit has its own lens and forms an image. The dragonfly's brain merges the many images into one highly detailed picture of its surroundings. Compound eyes are especially good at picking up something that is moving.

Do you know...?

Dragonflies are the closest thing the natural world has got to a helicopter. The insects do not simply flap their wings, but twist them back and forth to create a little vortex, or whirlwind, that lifts the insect.

149

How can you tell the difference between a damselfly and a dragonfly?

A dragonfly rests with its wings laid flat.

Do you know...?

The biggest and meanest dragonflies of all are the hawkers (below). They have an amazing flying ability. As well as being some of the fastest insect flyers, they can hover and are even able to fly backwards!

Damselflies and dragonflies form a family of insects called the Odonata. Both types of insect have four long, narrow wings and a body with a flexible abdomen (rear section), They also have a large head equipped with powerful jaws and huge eyes. However, when you see the two types moving around, they begin to look very different. Dragonflies tend to be larger than damselflies. They are powerful flyers. And when resting, dragonflies lay their wings flat. Damselflies are slower flyers than their cousins. They can only catch prey that are also bad flyers. In contrast to dragonflies, damselflies rest with their wings held upright.

Which are the longest insects?

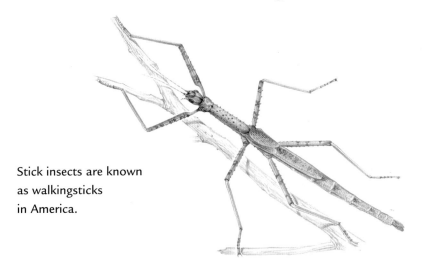

Stick insects are known
as walkingsticks
in America.

With their long and narrow bodies, it is not surprising that stick insects are the longest insects in the world. The record holder is a female stick insect from Malaysia. She grew to 33 centimetres long – imagine an insect that is longer than your school ruler!

Stick insects are not stick shaped by accident. They are pretending to be pieces of wood. Some even have spikes on their bodies, so they look like twigs from thorn bushes. If danger is near, the insects stand completely still. Most predators would have a tough time finding them among all the twigs.

Do you know...?

Stick insects have close relatives called the leaf insects. While most stick insects have no wings, leaf insects use theirs to make their wide, flat bodies more leaf shaped (right). Leaf insects will even sway in the breeze, like a leaf, to avoid being spotted by an attacker.

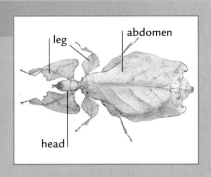

leg

abdomen

head

Why do ants collect stick-insect eggs?

Many stick insects are born in ant nests.

Female stick insects lay their eggs close to plants that their nymphs (young) will feed on.

In many cases, an ant will come along and carry the stick-insect egg back to its nest. The growing nymph is not in any danger. Its egg has a very hard outer coating, which the ants cannot get into. The ants are more interested in a food parcel called a capitulum, which is attached to the egg. Once this is cut off, the ants leave the egg alone. It is safe in the nest from attack by wasps and fungi. Once it hatches, the ants let the nymph crawl out of the nest to feed.

Do you know...?

If a predator sees through a stick insect's disguise, the insect has one more line of defence. It squirts a nasty liquid in the attacker's face. The spray blinds the attacker for a short time, while the insect (below) escapes.

Do earwigs ever get into your ears?

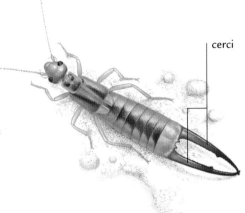

cerci

An earwig is easy to identify by the pincers, or cerci, at the back of the body.

Nobody really knows where the name earwig came from. Word experts know that the name is the Old English for 'ear insect', but that does not explain why the animals are named this. Many people think that earwigs crawled into people's ears. But is that because of their name or for another reason? Whatever the answer, earwigs do not live in, or even visit, people's ears or the ears of any other animals.

Like other insects, earwigs have cerci (spikes) growing out of their rear ends. However, an earwig's cerci are shaped into pincers, which can give a little nip. Earwigs spend most of their time on the ground. Some species have no wings at all. Earwigs are scavengers – they eat dead bodies and other waste.

Do you know...?

A few earwigs have become specialist scavengers. They live on the bodies of bats and rats, as well as eating their own poo and dead skin. These earwigs (below) have flat bodies, no wings and only tiny cerci.

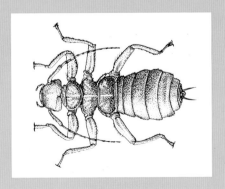

How do earwigs look after their children?

Earwigs make good parents.

Most insects never meet their parents. The majority of insect parents are dead before their eggs have had a chance to hatch.

Earwigs are unusual insects because they are caring parents. The female digs a burrow for her eggs. Sometimes the male helps out but he is chased away before the female lays her eggs. She keeps the eggs clean and warm and nips anything that comes near with her pincers. Once the nymphs (young) hatch, their mother feeds them with scraps of food from outside the nest. Soon the nymphs collect their own food but return to the nest to rest. Eventually the young leave home entirely. After that their mother does not recognise them as her own.

Do you know...?

Both male and female earwigs have pincers. In most species the pincers of the males are longer than those of the females. The reason for the difference is that males must fight each other for mates. The pincers are also used in mating.

Do termites grow their own food?

Termites should not be confused with ants. Like ants, termites live in huge colonies. The members of the colony all work together to find food, care for the young and build the nest. However, termites are not all sisters as in a colony of ants. There are males working in the nest, too.

Many types of termite gather food, but some species farm food in gardens. These insects cannot digest (break down) plant food very well, so they feed plants to a fungus in 'gardens' inside their nest. The fungus is able to remove all the goodness from the food. The termites then harvest the fungus and eat that instead.

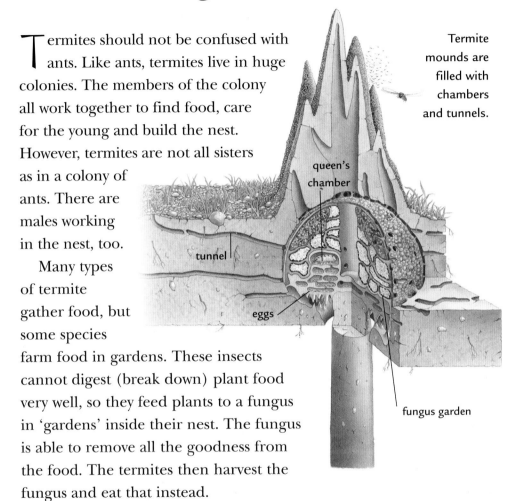

Termite mounds are filled with chambers and tunnels.

queen's chamber

tunnel

eggs

fungus garden

Do you know...?

Termites eat a wide range of foods, including dead wood. Wood-eating termites create tunnels and chambers in the wood, which they use as a nest. These termites can attack the wooden frames of houses and their feeding seriously weakens the buildings.

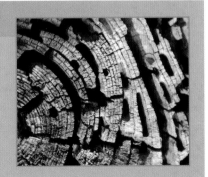

How do termites keep their mounds cool?

The largest termite mounds can get very hot inside as they are baked by the Sun day after day. The body heat from the thousands of termites living inside also increases the temperature. Termites build an air-conditioning system to stop their homes from over-heating. This system draws cool, fresh air into the mound from outside and pushes the hot, stale air out. The termites do this by building chimneys and cellars at the top and bottom of the mound. Warm air rises up the chimneys and out of the mound. This current of air draws in fresh air, which sinks down to the cellars. Down there, it is cool because of the damp soil. The system of warm air rising and cool air sinking creates a gentle breeze through the nest.

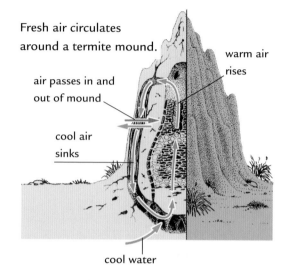

Fresh air circulates around a termite mound.

warm air rises

air passes in and out of mound

cool air sinks

cool water

Do you know...?

A termite mound is a natural skyscraper. Some stand for 100 years and contain millions of insects. The largest mounds are called termitaria (below). They can stand 9 metres high and a similar distance across. These huge nests also extend deep into the ground.

Are all the termites in a mound the same?

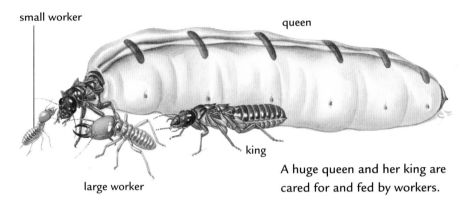

small worker

queen

king

large worker

A huge queen and her king are cared for and fed by workers.

A termite nest is ruled by a king and a queen. This pair are the mother and father of all the other termites in the colony. The queen is a massive egg-producing machine. She cannot move but sits in a room deep within the nest, where she produces 3,000 eggs a day. The king sits by her side. He is the second largest termite in the colony. All he does is mate with the queen. The royal couple control the nest by releasing chemical signals. They can live for 20 years.

The king and queen and all their young are cared for by workers. Workers are male or female. Small workers stay in the nest, cleaning the eggs and tending the fungus gardens. Large workers are equipped with big mouthparts. They collect food from outside.

Do you know...?

Some termites are soldiers. Their job is to protect the nest. They are larger than the workers. The soldiers of most species are armed with huge jaws. However, some (right) have nozzles instead of mouths. The nozzle is for squirting nasty chemicals at attackers.

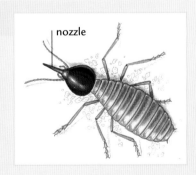

nozzle

Why is a hissing cockroach so noisy?

Hissing cockroaches are the noisiest members of the cockroach family. They get their name from the way the males can squeeze air out of the breathing tubes along the sides of their bodies. That produces loud hisses.

Hissing cockroaches produce these noises during battles for mates. A pair of males butt their heads together and try to push their rival away. They hiss loudly during the fights to show how strong they are. The males also hiss as they woo mates. A female will not mate with a male that cannot hiss.

The hissing cockroach is from the large African island of Madagascar.

Do you know...?

The world's smallest cockroach lives in North America. This tiny insect lives inside the nests of leaf-cutter ants (below), eating their food supplies. That makes it a pest for the ants, just as larger cockroaches are pests for us!

How do cockroaches eat wood?

Wood is not a tasty food. It is made from tough fibres called cellulose. No animal can digest (break down) cellulose. It would pass through a person's gut more or less unchanged.

However, several insects, including cockroaches, can survive by eating wood. Cockroaches also make do with paper and cardboard, which are made from wood fibres. They do not digest the wood themselves but have protozoa in their stomachs that can digest the wood for them. Protozoa are tiny life-forms made of just a single cell. They survive inside the cockroach by taking in some of the digested food, and the cockroach absorbs the rest of the food.

Cockroaches scavenge for food, including dead wood.

Do you know...?

The Pacific beetle cockroach does not lay eggs. It gives birth to young instead. The mothers feed their babies with a liquid 'milk' when they are inside her body.

Cockroaches will eat almost anything.

Will a female praying mantis eat her mate?

A praying mantis is a hunting insect. It catches its prey with its powerful spiked forelegs. These reach forwards to snatch a victim. When resting, the mantis holds its two weapons up in front as if it is praying – that is where the name comes from.

A praying mantis preys on smaller insects.

spiked forelegs

Female praying mantises are larger and fiercer than the males. It is often said that a female praying mantis will eat its mate. This is not normal behaviour, but every now and then an unlucky male gets mistaken for a meal rather than a mate. The female might allow a male to mate, but he is still not safe. Halfway through she forgets who the male is and decides to chew off his head!

Do you know...?

Male praying mantises produce mating 'calls'. That ensures they meet only females who want to mate. The call is in the form of a smelly message. The insect spreads this signal by flapping his wings.

How does a mantis make a nest from foam?

A female praying mantis needs a safe place for her eggs. She makes an egg case – called an ootheca – out of foam. The foam is produced from a liquid made by glands on the insect's abdomen (rear end). The mantis attaches a blob of foam to a twig. While the foam is still soft and wet, the female mantis makes several small chambers inside the blob. She then lays a single egg inside each chamber. After a while, the foam hardens into a material a bit like polystyrene. That keeps the egg safe.

Mantis nymphs climbing down from their nest on a silk rope.

Do you know...?

Mantis nymphs (young) climb out of the ootheca through a one-way door. The nymphs (right) look similar to adults except they have no wings. When small, some mantis nymphs pretend to be ants and hide in their nests.

Why do stoneflies drum?

Adult stoneflies find their mates at night in a curious way. They take up position on a plant leaf near to a stream. First the male drums the leaf to send out vibrations through the plant. A female will pick up the vibrations and drum back. The male then crawls to where he thinks the sound is coming from. He checks by drumming again. Eventually the two track each other down. After mating, the female lays eggs in the stream.

A European stonefly.

Do you know...?

A stonefly nymph (young) changes into an adult in many steps. After each stage it moults, or sheds its skin. With each moult, the nymph is slightly different. Stoneflies go through about 24 forms, or instars, before becoming adults. The final instar (right) then climbs out of the water and changes into an adult.

Why are thrips known as thunderbugs?

A thrips or thunderbug, bigger than life size.

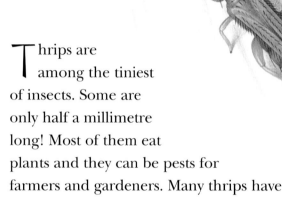

Thrips are among the tiniest of insects. Some are only half a millimetre long! Most of them eat plants and they can be pests for farmers and gardeners. Many thrips have wings, but even those who do not still travel by air. They are so tiny that the insects are swept along by the wind and fall to ground a long way away. The thrips often arrive in the winds that blow before a thunderstorm. For that reason, they are known as thunderbugs.

Watch out, there will be thrips about!

Do you know...?

Although it sounds a bit funny, the word *thrips* is both singular and plural – just like the words *sheep* or *deer*. So you can have one thrips or one million thrips. The name does not change.

Do booklice really eat books?

A booklouse.

Booklice are small wingless insects. They have been around much longer than books, and in the wild they eat rotten leaves and wood. They are expert chewers and can swallow just about any type of food.

Booklice have now learned to live in buildings. They get their name from their appetite for the glue used in old books. This glue contained substances from plants that the insects could feed on. It was common to come across some booklice when taking a book from a dusty library shelf. Today, books are glued with chemicals, so booklice normally leave books alone.

Do you know...?

Booklice are tiny creatures. Most are just a few millimetres long. However, they are often attacked by a wasp that is even smaller. The male wasps are just 0.14 millimetres long, which makes them the smallest insects ever discovered. The female wasps lay eggs in booklice eggs.

Booklice would love to live here.

Why do male webspinners have floppy wings?

A female webspinner does not have any wings.

Webspinners are little insects that live in warm parts of the world. Most species are just a few millimetres long. They live in forests and rocky places where they can feed on moss and fallen leaves. The adults build a network of tunnels under bark or among pebbles. The insects live in these tunnels along with their nymphs (young). The tunnels are camouflaged with bits of leaf and bark, so the little silk houses are often difficult to spot.

Female webspinners never leave the tunnels. They collect food through doors in the silk. The males have wings and fly between nests. However, running back and forth through the tunnels is difficult with stiff wings. So the male webspinners pump blood out of them until they go floppy. Floppy wings do not get stuck in the silk.

Do you know...?

It is not unusual for insects to produce silk. Many types of larvae (young insects) use it to build a protective cocoon. However, these insects produce silk from their abdomens (rear ends). Webspinners have silk glands on their forelegs. That allows them to build a silky tunnel while still moving forwards.

Which insect transmits more diseases than any other?

Have you ever had head lice? It is nothing to worry about if you have. Just about everyone gets them at some time or other. Head lice make tiny bites in skin to drink your blood. Sometimes they spread to other parts of the body. It makes you itchy just thinking about it!

A head louse crawls through hair.

Head lice are less common now than in the past. That is partly because we are all a bit cleaner. But it is also because we all live in larger houses. Lice love a crowd so they can move from one person to another.

Head lice are not entirely harmless. They infect the blood with diseases – more than any other insect. In places without good hospitals, the lice even spread fatal illnesses, such as typhus.

Do you know...?

All animals suffer with lice. Birds suffer more than most, such as the ostrich (below). Lice make the birds itch – a lot! It is difficult to scratch without hands, so the birds take dust baths – a roll in dry soil – to relieve themselves.

What do young lacewings use to disguise themselves?

Lacewing larvae are fierce little hunters. They feast on insect eggs and prey on small insects such as aphids. They suck the insides out of prey. But they do not throw the empty husks away. Instead, they strap them to their backs along with bits of moss. These objects are held in place by hooked hairs, and they make the lacewing look like a pile of rubbish. That makes the perfect disguise for creeping up on unsuspecting prey!

Most adult lacewings are small, fragile insects.

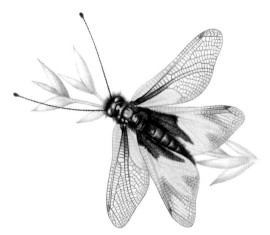

This colourful relative of lacewings is called a butterfly lion.

Do you know...?

Lacewings lay their eggs on leaves. Rather than attach them to the surface of the leaf, the female places them on top of a stalk of hard mucous. The stalks protect the eggs from their brothers and sisters, which would eat any eggs that were within reach!

167

Where do alderflies lay their eggs?

A European alderfly.

Adult alderflies are small flying insects that live near to water. Their larvae (young) live under water. The males find mates by beating their abdomens against a leaf to send vibrations to females nearby. After mating, the female finds a rock on the riverbank or a plant that hangs over the water. She lays her eggs in neat rows. Together the little eggs form a mat, or sheet. Smaller species lay a few hundred eggs, while larger ones produce a mat of 3,000 eggs.

Do you know...?

As soon as they hatch, alderfly larvae head for the water. Most will spend the next year in the water, preying on other young insects. Some species take longer to develop into adults and stay in the water for five years. In places where rivers dry out (right), the larvae crawl into a damp place, such as under a rock, until the water comes back.

How did the snakefly get its name?

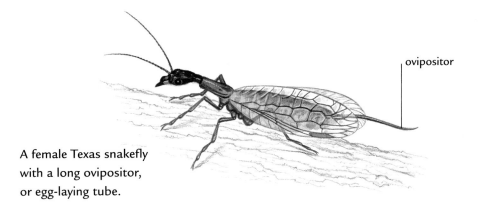

ovipositor

A female Texas snakefly
with a long ovipositor,
or egg-laying tube.

Snakeflies are unusual insects that prey on smaller insects. They are stealthy hunters that creep up on their prey and grab them with a speedy thrust of the head. This attack motion looks the same as a strike by a snake. Insects do not really have a neck, so snakeflies use a flexible section called the thorax (mid-body) to move the head back and forth.

The real thing!

Do you know...?

When an insect larva (young), is ready to make the change into an adult, it will take on a halfway stage, called a pupa. A familiar pupa is the chrysalis of a butterfly. The pupae of butterflies and most other insects are not able to move. However, the pupae of snakeflies are able to crawl about. They wriggle into cracks in logs. If the log is put on a fire, the pupae make a run for it!

How do caddisflies use fishing nets?

Young caddisflies live underwater. They eat mainly the remains of dead plants and they also scrape algae (minute plant-like organisms) off pebbles. This way of feeding requires the larvae (young) to move around a lot.

However, some caddisfly larvae have come up with a way of collecting food while staying still. They spin a net of silk threads and attach it to the stream bed in a place where the water current runs through it. Some nets are tubes, others are spirals, while another design is a network of tubes. The silk filters algae and other floating foods out of the water for the larvae to eat. Some larvae actually live in the net, while others shelter nearby.

An adult great red sedge rests on the stem of a water plant.

Do you know...?

Most caddisfly larvae do not build nets. Instead, they make themselves houses out of shells and plants. The insect pulls its case around using a hook on its abdomen (rear section). These larval cases give the insect somewhere to hide from predators. Even when it is feeding on the sandy bed of a stream far from stones or plants, the insect can disappear from sight when attacked.

Why do scorpionflies give their mates a ball of dried saliva?

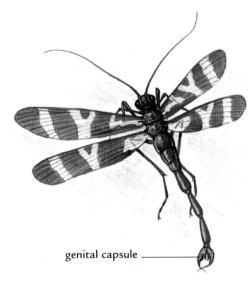

genital capsule

Only a male scorpionfly has the pointed genital capsule on its tail that makes it look like a scorpion.

Do you know...?

As their name would suggest, hangflies (below) spend a lot of their time hanging from leaves. The males attract mates by hanging with a wedding gift of freshly killed prey. However, other males often pretend to be females and steal the gift so they can attract their own mates.

Scorpionflies are named after the shape of the male's abdomen (rear section). It looks like the sting on the tail of a scorpion. The object is not a sting but is used for mating.

A male scorpionfly has to work hard to attract a mate. First he will catch a small fly or other insect to give to his mate as a wedding present. He wraps the gift in silk and releases a chemical signal to let the female know he is ready. If the male cannot catch a gift, he makes one out of a ball of dried saliva. Most females prefer a tastier treat, but eventually the male's gift of saliva will be accepted.

If a flea was as big as a man, how high could it jump?

A flea jumps from a 'kneeling' position.

Fleas are the high-jump champions of the natural world. They can jump off the ground to a height of about 80 times their own height and make leaps that are 150 times their body length. That is the equivalent of a man that is 1.8 metres tall being able to jump about 140 metres into the air and land 270 metres away! That means he could jump over Wembley Stadium arch and land two-thirds of the way up the pitch!

Fleas need to jump this high so that they can leap onto passing animals. These insects live on the blood and skin of large animals, such as mammals and birds. Pets, such as dogs and cats, often carry fleas – and fleas like living on people, too!

Do you know...?

Fleas may be expert jumpers but they are hopeless at landing. They cannot control which part of their body hits the ground first and normally make a crash landing. Because they are so light, they do not get hurt.

How did fleas kill a third of the people in Europe?

The black rat brought fleas and the plague to Europe from India.

In the middle of the 14th century a terrible disease swept across Europe. It was known then as the Black Death, but today we know it as bubonic plague. Within 50 years, one-third of the people of Europe – 25 million people – had died from the disease.

The disease was spread by black rats, which had arrived in Europe from Asia. The rats carried fleas, which in turn had plague bacteria in their stomachs. Rat fleas do not normally bite people, but those with the plague had their throats blocked by the bacteria multiplying inside them. That made the fleas so hungry they bit into any animal – including people – and passed on the disease.

Do you know...?

Bubonic plague is now a rare disease and it can be treated with medicines. But the fleas and bacteria are still out there. One animal with fleas that carry the plague are groundhogs (right). They are large squirrels that live in burrows in the south-western United States.

Do millipedes have a thousand legs?

A giant millipede, which can grow to 30 centimetres in length.

The name *millipede* means 'a thousand feet'. Millipedes certainly do have a great many legs – far more than six like an insect or eight like a spider. Millipedes belong to an entirely different group of animals from those two. They are myriapods, another name that refers to the way millipedes look. It means 'many feet'.

However, even the largest millipedes do not have 1000 legs. The maximum number of legs is about 750 (375 along each side), but most millipedes have about 200 legs.

A millipede manages to fit in so many legs because its body contains dozens of segments. These join to make the animal very long. Each segment has two pairs of legs.

Do you know...?

Millipedes walk by moving their many legs in waves along their bodies. Most of the legs are touching the ground, but in three or four places along the body, the legs are being lifted up and forwards to pull the millipede's body along.

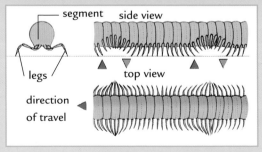

segment   side view

legs

direction of travel

top view

Which is the longest centipede?

The house centipede, a common hunter in the home.

Centipedes are another member of the myriapods, along with millipedes and several other types of long-bodied creature. The name centipede means 'a hundred feet', but most have only about 40 feet. Unlike millipedes, centipedes have just one pair of legs on each of their body segments.

Another difference from plant-eating millipedes is that centipedes are fierce killers. The fiercest killers of all are also the largest centipedes. They are called Scolopendra (right) and can grow to 30 centimetres. These giants can give a painful bite, and their venom (poison) is strong enough to make a child seriously ill.

Do you know...?

Centipedes kill by pumping a venom into prey through fangs. At least, fangs is what we call them. But these fangs are not teeth. They are not even in the mouth or on the head! Instead, a centipede's fangs are located on the first body segment.

CHAPTER 9
SPIDERS

Are spiders a type of insect?

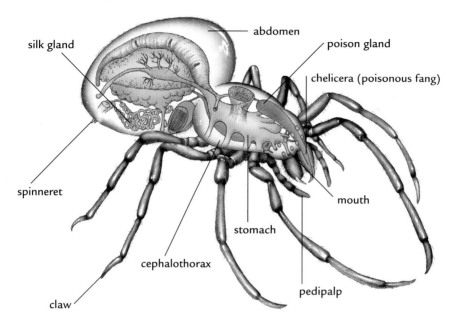

silk gland

abdomen

poison gland

chelicera (poisonous fang)

spinneret

mouth

stomach

cephalothorax

claw

pedipalp

The body of a spider, inside and out.

After flies and wasps, spiders are probably the most common creepy-crawlies to be seen in people's houses. For many people, they are unwelcome visitors to their homes, but they do a lot of good. Without spiders there would probably be a lot more flies in your house!

It is hard to get spiders and insects mixed up. The two are very different-looking animals. All insects have six legs and many have wings. Spiders never have wings and all have eight legs. An insect's body is divided into three sections. A spider has just two. The head and 'chest' form the front section, the cephalothorax. The larger rear section is the abdomen.

Do you know...?

Spiders may not be insects, but that does not stop some species pretending to be. Some little spiders pretend to be ants. They lift up their front legs so they look like antennae (feelers). They use this disguise to make hunting raids on ants' nests.

Is spider's silk stronger than steel?

This might sound like an odd question. A spider's web is ripped apart by a duster while a steel bridge can support hundreds of lorries and cars. But think again. The silk used to make a web is incredibly thin. If a steel wire was made that thin it would not be able to hold the weight of the spider and its prey. And if a bridge was made from spider's silk, it could carry even more traffic – but still be lighter than a steel structure!

A single silk strand supports the whole weight of a spider.

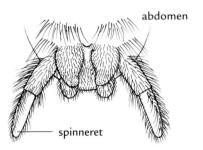

abdomen

spinneret

A line of silk is made from liquid squeezed through holes in spinnerets on a spider's rear.

Do you know...?

Orb web spiders make a web according to a set plan. They start by making a 'Y' shape (1). They then add spokes (2) and a spiral of silk (3, 4).

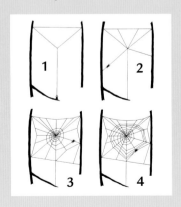

1

2

3

4

How do tarantulas fire poison darts?

Have you ever scared a tarantula? You would remember if you had. The frightened spider tilts its body backwards and throws its front legs up. This movement shows off the spider's immense fangs.

If that is not enough to scare an attacker off, the spider points its abdomen at the threat and vibrates its legs on a section of the abdomen. This area is covered in tiny hairs, which are rubbed off and thrown towards the attacker. The hairs have barbed tips – like an angler's hook – which are coated in poison. The hairs stick into the skin and sting like a nettle. If a hair dart gets stuck in the eye or lip the pain can be excruciating.

Tarantulas are very hairy spiders. They are also known as baboon spiders.

Do you know...?

The name *tarantula* itself has an interesting history. The word comes from the southern Italian city of Taranto. A large spider in that area is called a tarantula by local people. This is actually a wolf spider and not related to the tarantula group – but the name became used for other hairy spiders. Italians do a whirling dance called the tarantella – meaning 'little tarantula' – in which the dancers form a spinning wheel shape.

Which is the largest spider?

The world's largest spider is called the goliath tarantula. This monster lives in the rainforests of South America, where it hunts for birds, mice and frogs. They kill these prey with their huge poisonous fangs.

The goliath tarantula males are larger than the females – it is usually the other way around in spiders. The males measure 30 centimetres from the tip of a leg to the tip of the one opposite.

Despite being so large, the goliath tarantula is a good climber. It hunts mainly in tree tops. The spiders have sticky pads on the tips of their legs, which allow them to climb up slippery surfaces – even glass and metal.

Do you know...?

The world's smallest spider lives in Samoa in the South Pacific. It is an orb web spider and grows to just 0.43 millimetres long. It could sit on the head of a pin.

The goliath tarantula would have no problem covering a dinner plate.

Which is the deadliest spider?

Spiders kill with venom – a poison that is pumped into a victim through fangs. Most spider venom has no effect on humans – and spider fangs are too tiny to get through the skin. However, some species can hurt people. Hairy monsters like tarantulas actually have a bite about as powerful as a bee sting. The species with the most powerful venom is the Sydney funnel-web spider from Australia. This is only a little spider, growing to 1.5 centimetres long.

Sydney funnel-webs produce a venom called atraxotoxin. The males produce six times as much venom as the females. During the breeding season, the males travel far and wide in search of a mate. At that time they are rather grumpy and bite easily. Medicine is available to stop the venom, so only 15 people have died in the last 60 years.

A Sydney funnel-web spider.

Do you know...?

The Brazilian wandering spider (below) kills more people than any other. Its venom is less powerful than other spiders but the Brazilian species bites very easily. The spider often enters houses and also travels the world in crates of bananas.

Do spiders ever throw nets over prey?

The spiders you see at home and in gardens catch flying insects in their webs. But a small group of spiders from Australia use webs to snare insects on the ground. The colourfully named ogre-faced spiders spin a small web between the tips of their four front legs. They hang on a single thread from a branch so they are positioned just above the ground.

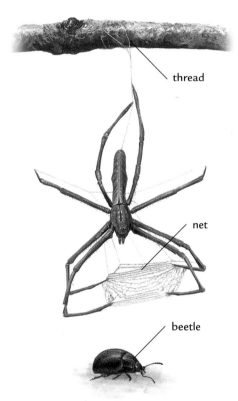

An ogre-faced spider prepares to catch a beetle in its silken net.

Do you know...?

The bolas spider lassos its prey. This spider preys on moths and lowers a ball of sticky silk on a rope from a branch. The ball is coated in chemicals that make a moth think it is a potential mate. The spider swings the ball in the air. When a moth arrives it gets stuck to the silk. The bolas spider then reels in its helpless victim.

The spiders are named after a pair of huge eyes, which let them see very well at night. When a beetle wanders under the motionless hunter, the spider stretches its net-like web wide and covers the beetle. The beetle gets tangled in the sticky silk as the net springs back to its original size.

Do all spiders spin webs?

A web is not very useful under the ground, and that is where a trap-door spider lives. This spider is an expert digger and builds itself a burrow using a rake-shaped mouthpart.

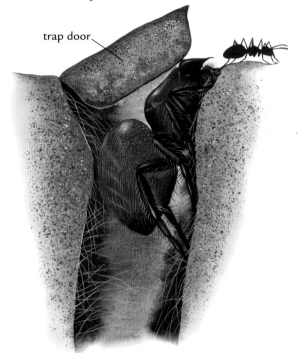

trap door

A trap-door spider about to snatch an ant.

The entrance of the burrow is sealed with a hinged door. The door is made of silk, sometimes with soil mixed in.

The spider spends its days sitting just under the trap door. It holds the door shut and wedges its body against the burrow wall. It is difficult to open the door if the spider does not want you to.

The spider can feel the vibrations of passing insects on the surface. When a victim comes close enough, the spider throws open the trap door with lightning speed and drags the insect inside. The door slams shut behind it.

How do nursery-web spiders protect their young?

Baby spiders live in their nursery web.

Many spiders look after their young, or spiderlings. Nursery-web spiders are among the most caring of parents. The female lays her eggs in a silken bag, or egg sac. She carries this package under her body everywhere she goes. It is so large that she has to walk on tiptoe. She carries the sac with her fangs, so she cannot eat until the eggs hatch. When that happens, the spider builds her spiderlings a nursery made of a funnel of silk. The mother stands guards over the nursery.

Do you know...?

Female lace weaver spiders (right) only live for two years. They mate in the first year but only produce two sets of eggs the year after. Then the spider dies. Once they hatch, the young spiderlings make use of their mother's dead body – they eat it!

Can spiders chew?

Spiders have powerful mouthparts. They are a pair of pointed fangs, known as chelicerae, which the spider sticks into prey during an attack. The fangs deliver a venom (poison) that either kills the prey or just paralyses it so it cannot escape.

However, the fangs cannot cut up the food into small

Do you know...?

Spitting spiders catch prey by squirting sticky goo over their prey. The spider sprays two zigzags of spit, which glues its victims to the ground. Then the spider kills its prey with a poisonous bite.

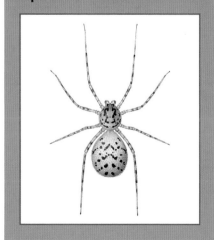

A fly is killed by a wolf spider.

chunks, and the spider has no teeth for chewing up its meal. So the spider pumps the contents of its stomach into its prey's body. Most animals digest (break down) food after they have swallowed it, but a spider does it the other way around. The spider's stomach juices work outside the body. They digest the insides of the prey into a fleshy soup. The spider then sucks up this tasty goo, leaving the prey's body as an empty husk.

How does a two-tailed spider tie up its prey?

Spiders do not have tails, so where do the two-tailed spiders get their name from? They are a small group of spiders that appear to have two tails sticking out from their abdomens (rear sections). However, these are a pair of very long spinnerets – the body parts that make the spider's silk.

long spinnerets

A two-tailed spider with its long spinnerets.

The long spinnerets are not used for weaving a web but for lashing prey to the ground. The spider waits on a trunk or rock for an insect to wander past. It then jumps over the prey, trailing a pair of sticky silken ropes from its 'tails'. It then runs around the victim wrapping it up in a tangle of silk.

Do you know...?

The name daddy-long-legs is used for several minibeasts. In Britain, we use it for the large insects we see fluttering around in summer. They are crane flies. However, the name is also used for harvestmen, relatives of spider with very long legs. To add to the confusion the name also applies to a group of spiders. Some of them, such as the cellar spider (right) make their way into homes.

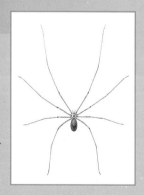

If a jumping spider was as large as you, how far could it leap?

Jumping spiders are tiny hunters. The largest are just 1.8 centimetres long and there are some species that are just 3 millimetres long.

Being small does not mean the spiders are not good at catching prey. They perch on a twig

A jumping spider.

Do you know...?

Jumping spiders need to be able to see very well so they can spot prey in the distance and judge exactly how far to jump. They have a total of eight eyes. The largest pair at the front are used to judge leaps. One eye alone is bigger than the spider's brain.

connected by a safety line of silk. When prey comes within striking distance, the spider launches itself onto it.

Jumping spiders can make truly enormous leaps. A spider that is less than a centimetre long can cover 20 centimetres in a single bound. If it was as big as you it would be able to jump more than 120 metres, or twice the length of a jumbo jet.

How do huntsmen spiders stay out of sight?

A small huntsman spider hides out on a leaf.

Huntsmen spiders ambush their prey. They lie in wait on a tree trunk or leaf, normally with their heads facing down. They sit motionless, but ever ready to strike with their long fangs.

Huntsmen spiders are difficult to see when they are waiting for prey. They have flat bodies that sit very close to the surface of their hiding places. That keeps any shadows that might give away the spider's position to a minimum. The legs also have a fringe of hairs that helps them blend into the background.

Do you know...?

The crab spider is another master of disguise. It lurks unseen on flowers for insects to arrive for a feed (below). The spider's body is coloured to match the flower, which makes it very difficult for the insects – and people – to spot.

Do any spiders feed their young on milk?

As its name suggests, the mothercare spider spends a long time looking after its babies. Females of this European species stay with their spiderlings (young) after they have hatched out. The spiderlings can get a meal from their mother by tugging on her legs. She produces food from her stomach. This 'spider milk' is a mixture of half-digested

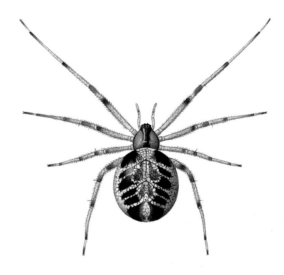

The female mothercare spider belongs to a family called the comb-footed spiders.

insects and the lining of the mother's stomach. When the spiderlings are a little larger, their mother brings them an insect to eat. The baby spiders are too small to bite into the insect themselves, so their mother punctures holes in the prey for them to eat through.

Do you know...?

A spider's eggs are at risk of attack from wasps, which lay their eggs inside the spider. The mothers of funnel weaver spiders (right) protect their eggs and spiderlings in a complex maze of silk. The maze is made up of many twisting tunnels. Unless you know the way through, it takes a while to find the eggs.

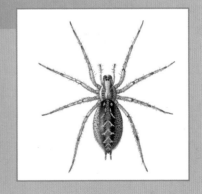

How do water spiders breathe under water?

Spiders seem to do well in most places, from dry grasslands to wind-swept mountain sides and damp caves. However, only one species lives in water. The European water spider hunts for fish, tadpoles and underwater insects.

Water spiders cannot breathe underwater – they have to take a supply of air with them. They build a 'diving bell' out of silk. This silk dome contains a bubble of air. The spider sits inside the diving bell with its legs hanging in the water to feel for prey. When it attacks, the spider climbs down into the water, but a silver bubble of air surrounds it and keeps it connected to the diving bell.

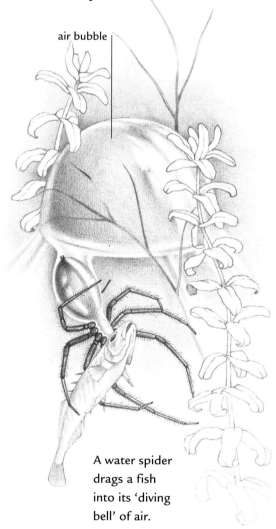

air bubble

A water spider drags a fish into its 'diving bell' of air.

Do you know...?

Several spiders hunt on the surface of water. They include the fisher spider and the pirate spider. They 'fish' by reaching across the water with their front legs. The back legs stay on the bank or on a floating leaf. The spider can feel the ripples made by insect prey in the water.

What does a wedding-present spider give his bride?

The wedding-present spider is a type of nursery-web spider from Europe, Asia and North Africa. Like other nursery-webs, the females of the species must work hard to raise their young. They carry eggs in an egg sac and then raise the spiderlings in a specially built silken nursery.

The males have to put some effort in too. Before a female lets a male mate with her, he has to give her a wedding present. The male catches a juicy fly, or similar insect, and gift wraps it in silk. He then approaches a female in a hunched position – almost kneeling as if proposing marriage. If the female ignores him, he waggles the gift until she accepts it. The female then eats her free meal during mating.

egg sac

A female wedding-present spider with her precious egg sac.

Do you know...?

Perhaps male black widow spiders should give their mates a present. These deadly spiders get their name from the story that the female (below) kills the males after mating — thus becoming a widow. However, it is just a story; most males survive.

How does a male house spider serenade its mate?

A male house spider makes a long quest to find the web of a mate.

Have you ever seen a spider with long, hairy legs creeping about your house? It is probably a male house spider searching for a female to mate with. Once he locates a web with a mate inside, he has to be careful. Even though he is only a little smaller than the female, he cannot walk into her web without announcing his arrival. The male tugs on the funnel-shaped web, sending a code of vibrations through it. The female inside knows that a male of her own species is outside and will not attack him if he climbs into her web to mate.

Do you know...?

Some jumping spiders prey on other spiders in their own webs. The spider climbs into the web without alerting its owners. When in position, the spider jiggles the web to fool its victims into walking across to see if some prey has flown into the web – straight into an ambush!

Why doesn't a spider get caught in its own web?

Spider webs are amazing pieces of construction. The large spiral shaped webs take several hours to produce and have to be rebuilt almost every day.

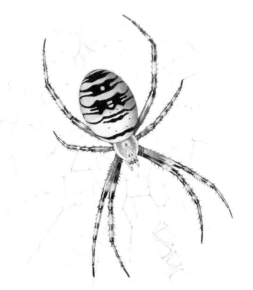

A wasp spider is an orb-weaver, some of the best web builders in the spider world.

When prey flies into a spider's web it has little chance of escape. The super-strong silk does not break under their weight, just stretches. The silk is coated with sticky liquid, which glues the prey to the web. The more the prey struggles, the more tangled up it gets. The spider at the centre of the web feels the impact and scuttles over to kill its victim. It does not get stuck on its own web because it has included some strands of non-sticky silk in the web. The spider is careful to only walk on them.

How do money spiders fly?

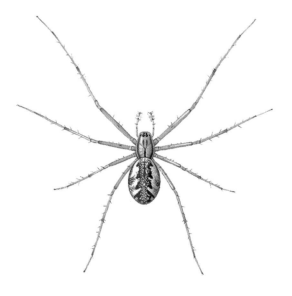

Money spiders are small spiders that live on bushes.

According to tradition, money spiders are good luck. The story goes that if one of them runs across your body when you are lying on the ground outside, it has come to spin new clothes for you because you are about to get a lot of money. Unfortunately that is not true, but something just as incredible is – money spiders can fly!

A family of spiderlings can contain more than 100 brothers and sisters, and they all need somewhere to live. It takes a long time to travel on foot, especially if you have eight like a spider does. It is much faster for young spiderlings to disperse by air. They do not have wings, so they 'balloon' instead. The tiny spiders produce strands of thin silk from their abdomens. These catch the wind, which carries the spiders for many miles.

Do you know...?

Another name for money spiders is gossamer spiders. Gossamer is a shiny but very thin and light material, and the spiders get this name because they weave very fine webs (below), that shimmer like gossamer in the morning dew.

CHAPTER 10
OTHER ARACHNIDS

Do scorpions kill prey with stings?

A scorpion shows off its weapons, front and rear.

Scorpions are known for their scary-looking stings on the tips of their tails. However, they are also armed with huge pincers, or pedipalps, at the front of their bodies. The pincers are the weapon of choice when the scorpion is hunting. The sting is usually used to fight off attacks, and the scorpion rarely wastes precious venom on prey.

Do you know...?

Every year thousands of people are stung by scorpions. But only about 20 species pose a danger to humans. Most scorpion stings are as harmless as a bee or a wasp sting.

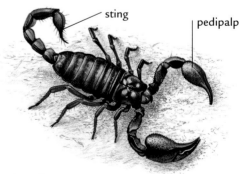

sting

pedipalp

The African emperor scorpion.

What is the difference between a pseudoscorpion and a scorpion?

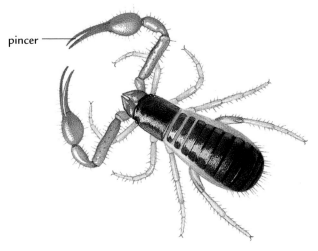

pincer

The word *pseudo* means 'fake' – so don't be fooled, pseudoscorpions are not scorpions. Instead they are a totally different type of arachnid. Pseudoscorpions are a much smaller type. The largest are less than a centimetre long. The smallest scorpion is four times that size. However, the two animals share some features. They both have eight legs, and, like the scorpions, pseudoscorpions have pincers, which they use for killing small insects. However, pseudoscorpions never have the same flexible tails and sting as their larger cousins.

This pseudoscorpion from Europe lives in moss and under bark.

Do you know...?

Pseudoscorpions are too small to travel far on their own. So they hitch rides on large animals. They grab hold of the hairs on flies and bees with their pincers. The relationship is often a close one. A pseudoscorpion from South America rides on a female beetle to new egg-laying sites in the wood of decaying fig trees.

How do scorpions look after their young?

A new family of scorpions goes for a walk.

Despite being ruthless killers, scorpions have a caring side. Young scorpions are very well looked after. The females do not lay eggs. Instead, they raise babies inside the body, keeping them fed as they grow for up to a year. When they are born, the tiny young scorpions are protected by their mother. She carries the young on her back.

Do you know...?

Scorpions are wary of their mates. One wrong move and they might get a fatal sting. So the pair perform an elaborate dance (below) to protect themselves from each other.

Why do harvestmen have detachable legs?

A harvestman is all legs.

Harvestmen are common arachnids. They are sometimes mistaken for spiders because they have eight legs. They get their name because they are often seen in autumn at harvest time.

Harvestmen have enormously long legs. With eight in total, a harvestman can afford to lose one or two in an emergency. If the arachnid comes under attack, one of its legs falls off and twitches. That lost limb is enough to occupy the attacker as the harvestman runs away.

Do you know...?

In most species of harvestman, the female leaves her eggs to their fate. A few mothers stay to babysit. But in one species, the father steps in to help. He builds a nest for the eggs and stands guard over them until they hatch.

How did the whip spider get its name?

Nobody can decide what to call members of this group. Biologists refer to them as the amblypigids, but that's too hard to say for everyone else. So what are they – whip spiders or tail-less whip scorpions? The arachnids are neither spiders nor scorpions. They have two obvious body sections, like a spider, but they also have powerful pincers for grabbing prey, similar to those of a scorpion.

At least the whip part of the name is more obvious. The whip spiders have a pair of extremely long front legs. They are not used for walking but as feelers. The whip scorpion swings its long legs around as it walks as if they were whips.

A pair of whip spiders.

Do you know...?

Whip spiders shed their skins at night. After the moult, the arachnid's new skin is very pale and soft (below left). Over the next few days, while its skin darkens and becomes hard, the arachnid hides away.

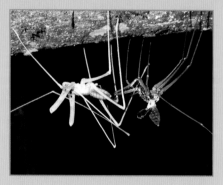

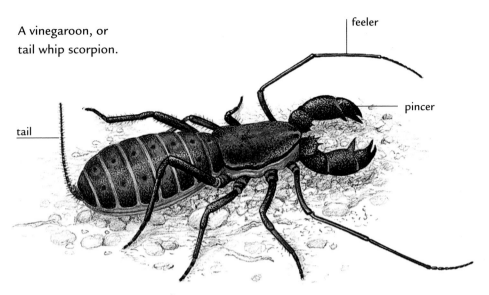

A vinegaroon, or tail whip scorpion.

feeler

pincer

tail

How does a vinegaroon squirt acid?

With a name like vinegaroon, it is no wonder that these little arachnids have a big reputation. There is no need to be frightened of them. All they can do to you is give you a little nip with their pincers. But a vinegaroon also has another weapon: its whip-like tail. When a vinegaroon feels under threat, it lashes out with this tail and sprays a weak acid from a gland at its base. The spray is largely made up of ascetic acid, a very mild substance more commonly known as vinegar. That is where the arachnid gets it name. Like whip spiders, the vinegaroon is active at night and walks on its six back legs. The front pair are long and flexible and are used as feelers in the dark.

Do you know...?

The microwhip scorpions are among the smallest of all arachnids. The largest reaches 2.5 millimetres in length. The smallest are only 0.5 millimetres when you discount their whip tails. Microwhip scorpions live deep in the soil. They have no eyes and lack the pincers of other whip scorpions.

How much does a tick expand after feeding?

A tick with a full stomach.

Ticks eat nothing but the blood of large animals, such as reptiles, birds and mammals. Ticks are found everywhere, from the deep oceans on the skin of a whale to seabirds in cold polar regions.

Very little stops a tick feeding. It has tough skin so it is not crushed if its host animal sits on it! The tick pushes its mouthparts right into skin. Its saliva stops the blood from forming a scab, and blood flows straight into its stomach. If you tried to pull a tick off your skin, the chances are you would rip it in two and leave its mouth stuck in you. Before it feeds, a tick is about 7 millimetres long. After a long drink of blood, it swells to 25 millimetres – three times the size!

Do you know...?

Ticks are arachnids, like scorpions and spiders. The adults have eight legs like their larger cousins. However, the tick larvae (young) have just six legs.

How do red spider mites move from plant to plant?

Red spider mites hitch a ride on the back of a fly.

R ed spider mites are serious pests. They often attack flowers. They are one of the few arachnids other than spiders that can make silk. They use their pincers, or pedipalps, to do this. They cover plants with webbing and drink the juice from the stems. That causes the plant to wilt and die.

Spider mites travel to new plants on the backs of insects that visit the flowers the mites live on. Large bees are often so weighed down with a cargo of mites that they have trouble taking off!

Do you know...?

There are three times as many female spider mites as males. Mating takes place on the host animal usually after they have had a meal. The males seek out young females that are about to turn into adults. They fight each other for access to the females. The winners guard their mates until each female is ready to mate.

203

Are ticks dangerous?

A tick that has been removed from the skin.

A tick bite is a nasty experience, but hopefully harmless. However, like other blood-sucking parasites, ticks can spread diseases. (A parasite is an animal that lives on another animal.)

When ticks bite, they squirt a little saliva into the wound to stop the blood from clotting into a scab. This saliva often contains disease-causing organisms, which pass into the bloodstream. The human diseases spread by ticks include Rocky Mountain fever, Lyme disease and tick-bite fever.

Do you know...?

The most dangerous disease passed on by tick bites is scrub typhus. The tick responsible is called the chigger, or red bug. These beasties live in Asia and the disease they spread can kill people.

You need to be careful of ticks in some places.

Which is the largest type of mite?

Most mites are incredibly small. They are only an eight-hundredth of a millimetre long – considerably smaller than the head of a pin. A giant among mites is the red velvet mite. This monster reaches 15 millimetres across, which is big for a mite. As their name suggests, red velvet mites are furry animals. They live in dry places such as grasslands but are out of sight most of the time. The best time to see these large mites is after rain, when they come out for a walk.

A red velvet mite.

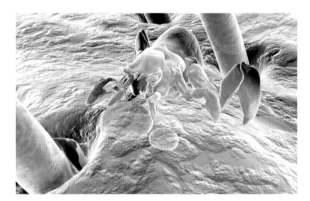

Most mites are tiny. This one is seen through a microscope.

Do you know...?

Gall mites are unusual members of the mite family. They have just four legs. They are named gall mites because they drink plant sap. In response to this attack, the plants form swellings, or galls. The galls provide a place for the mites to feed but stop them from damaging the plant.

Do mites cause allergies?

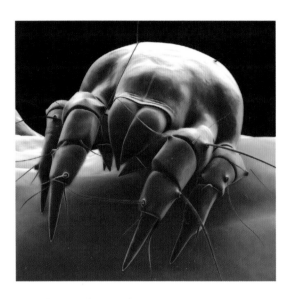

A dust mite feeds on dead skin.

Mites are among the most widespread animals on Earth. Experts estimate that there are 800,000 of them in a square metre of fallen leaves. They live in polar ice and swim in the deep ocean. Mites also live inside the 'ears' of moths and the breathing tubes of bees.

And mites also live in your house. Even the cleanest homes have dust mites living there. These tiny creatures are thought to be a major cause of sneezing and allergies that create breathing problems, such as asthma. People are allergic to the mites' waste.

Dust mites are everywhere.

Do you know...?

The scabies itch mite is passed through touching dirty skin. The mite burrows into the skin and that causes an itchy red rash that is especially bad around the hands and wrists.

Do sun spiders enjoy sunshine?

Sun spiders are also called wind scorpions.

At first glance, sun spiders look like they have ten legs. However, the first pair of 'legs' are really the animal's pedipalps. In most arachnids, the pedipalps form pincers, but in sun spiders they are sensitive feelers. They reach out in front of the animal as it moves and are not used for walking.

Sun spiders get their name from the hot and sunny places they live in. However, they stay hidden away during the day and come out at night.

A sun spider from Africa.

pedipalp

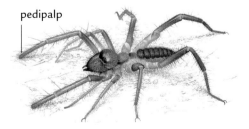

Do you know...?

Sun spiders do not need pincers because they have huge jaws. The spike-shaped mouthparts make up a third of the animal's body parts. Sun spiders prey on scorpions, mice and large insects.

Is a horseshoe crab actually a crab?

Horseshoe crabs come ashore to find mates.

Crabs belong to a large group of animals called the crustaceans. They share this group with shrimp, lobsters and krill. However, despite their name, horseshoe crabs are not included in the crustaceans. Instead, they form a group of animals – with just 4 species – called the Merostomata. This class is part of a larger collection of animals, called the chelicerates, which also includes the arachnids, such as spiders and ticks. So arachnids are the closest living relatives of horseshoe crabs. Horseshoe crabs live in the sea and feed on shellfish and worms. They are one of the few animals to have blue blood rather than red.

Do you know...?

Sea spiders (below) are one of the world's weirdest creatures. They form a group all of their own. Despite having eight legs, they are not closely related to spiders, insects or crustaceans.